Combat Aircraft Library

Helicopters

of the World

Contents

Combat Aircraft Library

Helicopters

of the World

Bill Gunston

TEMPLE PRESS
AEROSPACE

TEMPLE · PRESS

리리리리리리리리리

NEWNES·BOOKS

Published by Temple Press
an imprint of Newnes Books
84/88 The Centre, Feltham, Middlesex TW13 4BH, England
and distributed for them by
The Hamlyn Publishing Group Limited
Rushden, Northants, England

Produced by Stan Morse
Aerospace Publishing Ltd
10 Barley Mow Passage
London W4 4PH

© Aerospace Publishing Ltd 1983

Colour profiles and line diagrams © Pilot Press Ltd

First published 1983
Second Impression 1984

ISBN: 0 600 35058 4

All correspondence concerning the content of this volume should be addressed to Aerospace
Publishing Ltd. Trade enquiries should be addressed to Temple Press.

Printed in Italy

PICTURE ACKNOWLEDGEMENTS
The publishers would like to thank the following people and organisations for their help in
supplying photographs for this book.

Jacket front: Westland Helicopters. **Jacket back:** Hughes Helicopters. **Page 3:** Herman Potgieter.
13: US Air Force. **14:** US Air Force/US Air Force. **15:** MoD. **16:** Cinéma Vidéo des Armées
(PCVA)/Bell Helicopter Textron. **17:** Press Association. **19:** Aérospatiale. **20:** US Navy. **21:** US
Navy/Lt K.P. White via Lt Stewart Cooper. **26:** Press Association. **27:** US Navy. **29:** Aérospatiale/
Aérospatiale. **30:** Aérospatiale. **31:** US Navy. **35:** Westland. **37:** Sikorsky. **38:** Herman Potgieter. **39:**
Bell Helicopter Textron. **40:** Aérospatiale. **41:** Aérospatiale. **46:** US Navy. **48:** Bell Helicopter
Textron. **49:** Klaus Niska. **55:** US Army. **59:** US Navy. **60:** Hughes Helicopters. **61:** Hughes
Helicopters. **63:** Messerschmitt-Bölkow-Blohm. **66:** Aérospatiale. **67:** Westland. **70:** Asahi
Helicopter. **72:** Court Helicopters. **73:** Asahi Helicopter. **74:** Bell Helicopter Textron. **75:** Asahi
Helicopter. **76:** British Airways. **77:** Aérospatiale/Kawasaki. **78:** Tyrolean Airways/Aérospatiale.
79: Messerschmitt-Bölkow-Blohm/Asahi Helicopter. **80:** Sikorsky.

Early Days

Bearing in mind that small toy helicopters have been common for many hundreds of years, one might have expected this sort of flying machine to be the first heavier-than-air type to be perfected. In fact it has proved a long and hard struggle.

Few of man's inventions have proved as tantalizingly frustrating as the helicopter. Perhaps because of aerodynamically rotating seeds, such as those of the sycamore, men have experimented with rotary-wing devices for an estimated 2,000 years. Almost 500 years ago the great Leonardo da Vinci was not only sketching toy 'air gyroscopes' working in principle like a helicopter but also experimenting with models, and with large rulers 'whirling most rapidly through the air so that you will find your arm borne in the same direction and along the same axis as the plane of the ruler'. It seemed but a short step to the achievement of manned powered flight by means of rotary wings – but nothing could have been further from the truth.

Even after the internal-combustion engine became available at the turn of the present century, the early man-carrying helicopters that were powered by it proved to be most unruly beasts. They shook, shuddered and thumped up and down, and if they could they tipped on their side or simply broke. Even after another 30 years of toil the best helicopters were pathetic performers compared with even the lowest-powered of the fixed-wing aeroplanes. It is a matter of historical fact that high-speed jets were thundering through the sky before a single useful helicopter had been delivered to a customer.

Juan de la Cierva's dogged persistence in the face of prolonged problems at last began to bring rewards with his C-4, based on a wartime Hanriot fighter, seen here airborne on 9 January 1923. All his early autogyros (he called them Autogiros) had wings.

Helicopters of the World

Even today, when turbine engines have transformed the helicopter in both safety and performance, it still cannot fly faster than about 180 mph (290 km/h), which would be thought very poor for most fixed-wing machines. And its insurance premiums are still more than twice those for aeroplanes of equivalent size or capacity. But such things take second place behind the central fact that, unlike aeroplanes, helicopters can really *fly*. Aeroplanes can only keep rushing forwards, and they cannot get into the air at all without accelerating forwards over a long smooth stretch of ground or water. The helicopter can move in any direction it wishes; it can hover motionless as long as there is fuel in the tank, and can perform countless tasks and missions that no aeroplane could attempt.

The Cierva C.19 Mk III was typical of autogyros of the 1930 era. It was one of the first to have a drive from the engine to spin up the rotor before take-off.

The first helicopters

History ascribes the title of 'first helicopter' to two machines built quite near each other – but totally independently – in northern France in 1907. The first to get daylight under its wheels was the Breguet-Richet No. 1; the Breguet family had been the world's greatest clockmakers and today they are still famed for their aeroplanes, but this pioneer helicopter – which looked like 16 Wright biplanes in close formation – was judged not to have 'flown' because four big men held on at all times to keep it under control. So the claim for the first free flight goes to Paul Cornu, near Lisieux on 13 November 1907, just eight weeks after the first test of the Breguet. Cornu's machine looked like a cross between a modern Chinook helicopter and a perambulator, but its 24-hp (17.9-kg) Antoinette engine enabled it to hover well clear of the ground for about 20 seconds.

Dozens of other strange machines followed, but only one would look sensible to a modern helicopter engineer. In 1911, after much playing with models, Russian Boris N. Yuriev built an amazingly neat and well-conceived machine which weighed a mere 862 lb (391 kg) and was powered by a 70-hp (52-kW) Gnome rotary engine. Alone among its bizarre contemporaries this helicopter had only a single main rotor, with a belt to drive a second, smaller rotor at the tail with its axis horizontal to give side-thrust. The arrangement looks odd, but the tail rotor is needed to stop the fuselage from spinning under the main rotor in the opposite direction, in other words to react against the torque in the main drive shaft. It is not a perfect layout, but nobody has found a better, and today almost all helicopters are designed that way.

We do not know if Yuriev had much success, but he was for 40 years highly respected among Russian, and then Soviet, helicopter engineers. His compatriot Igor Sikorsky almost achieved success in 1909 and again in 1910, but then wisely dropped the idea and moved into the world of large aeroplanes and flying-boats. Igor Sikorsky was thus a famed aircraft designer when, in 1939, he returned to the more intractable problems of rotating wings.

Cierva (Avro) Rota Mk 1 of No. 529 Squadron, RAF, operating on radar calibration duties in 1943-4.

Before that happened more than 100 helicopters had been built in at least 19 countries, and more than 20 actually rose from the ground. Most looked extremely clumsy and complex to modern eyes, and not one was of any practical use.

There was, however, an interesting sidestreet of rotary-wing development which worked in a different way and produced quicker results. In Spain a leading aeroplane builder was Juan de la Cierva. Young and wealthy, he was a sound engineer and his inquiring mind sought an answer when in 1919 a test pilot crashed his giant 14-passenger 80-ft (24.4m) span transport by making too tight a turn at too low a speed. It stalled, prompting Cierva to start looking for a way to overcome the danger. He soon found that, to keep the wings always moving at a safe speed, they had to rotate. He decided to develop an autogyro (he spelt it 'Autogiro', and registered the name), which is essentially an aeroplane whose fixed wings are replaced by a free-spinning rotor. It takes off like an aeroplane, and at all times is pulled along by the thrust of its propeller or propellers, but the air flowing diagonally up through the rotor causes it to spin so that, with careful design, the blades give lift equally on both sides of the aircraft. Later autogyros could clutch-in the engine to spin the rotor and thus make a vertical take-off (VTO), but all have free-spinning rotors in flight through which the air flows diagonally upwards. This is the opposite to a helicopter, whose power-driven main rotor drives the air downwards.

Slow progress

On the face of it the idea of the helicopter, as a kind of flying machine lifted by a propeller turning about a vertical axis, could hardly be simpler. In practice it proved quite the opposite, except for the few helicopters whose objective was merely VTO, without any attempt to fly from one place to another. For example, in World War I the Austro-Hungarian artillery put into service a simple helicopter with coaxial (oppositely rotating about the same axis) rotors looking like large propellers driven by three rotary engines arranged around the machine at 120° intervals. It could never have

The Flettner Fl 282 Kolibri was the first mass-production helicopter, though Allied bombing wrecked dozens in the factories. This was the seventh of 30 prototypes ordered in 1941 together with the first 15 production machines. In 1942 it was one of nine used for trials from warships.

Helicopters of the World

The Focke-Achgelis Fa 61 was the first helicopter to be publicly demonstrated in fully controlled flight. It had a major influence on subsequent German, Russian and US designs.

been flown forwards under control, because there were no controls, except the throttle lever. But as it only had to go up and down it was used over a long period in 1916-17 until someone hit the ground at too high a rate of descent.

As soon as designers tried to make useful helicopters they found that their creations became awesomely complicated. The main rotor blades tended to have various hinges at the roots where they joined the hub, and to sprout hinged control surfaces on their trailing edge. Small auxiliary rotors, usually resembling propellers, often appeared at the nose, tail or on lateral outriggers to push up, down or to either side. Not only were the contraptions complicated, but they inevitably suffered from the most severe vibration. Unlike the aeroplane the helicopter was vitally dependent on power-driven shafting, bearings, gearboxes and blades, all highly stressed and while in flight apparently trying to shake themselves to pieces.

There was no sudden breakthrough. Progress was very gradual, and each new helicopter sometimes had a useful experimental life of several years but eventually had to be discarded. One of the original pioneers, Louis Breguet, teamed with his technical director René Dorand in 1932 to build a Gyroplan Laboratoire with coaxial rotors driven by a 350-hp (261-kW) radial in the nose. It flew in June 1935 after 18 months of tethered tests, and in a further 18 months set world helicopter records at 61 mph (98 km/h) speed, 518 ft (158 m) altitude, 27 miles (43 km) distance and 62 minutes duration. These figures were soon eclipsed by the German Focke-Achgelis Fa 61. Focke had built Cierva autogyros and used a similar approach in designing the Fa 61 in 1933-4. The main

Probably the first helicopter in the world put into mass production (in 1942), the Flettner

Fl 282 Kolibri saw quite wide active service with the German Luftwaffe and, especially, the Kriegsmarine, in 1943-4. This picture shows the 21st development prototype, almost identical to production Kolibris. With the rotors fore-and-aft the right rotor cannot be seen from this side.

difference was that he used two rotors side-by-side on braced outriggers and connected them to the 160-hp (119-kW) engine (which drove a small propeller to keep the cylinders cool). The Fa 61 flew in June 1936, and in February 1938 made headlines around the world when Hanna Reitsch demonstrated it impressively before a colossal Nazi gathering inside the Deutschlandhalle in Berlin. Later it set records at 76 mph (122 km/h) speed, 11,244 ft (3427 m) altitude and 143 miles (230 km) distance.

German developments

A parallel German machine built by the Flettner company also showed promise. Powered by a similar 160-hp (119-kW) engine, the Fl 185 of 1936 had only one main rotor but two propellers on the ends of outriggers looking like extremely narrow wings. Anton Flettner hoped to be able to make the machine fly like an autogyro in cruising flight, the drive to the main rotor being disconnected and all the power transferred to the propellers, but he encountered severe problems. By 1937 he was building true helicopters and these broke new ground in having intermeshing twin rotors. Popularly known as the 'eggbeater' arrangement, this configuration uses left and right main rotors

Flettner Fl 265 single-seat experimental helicopter in flight at Johannisthal aerodrome about 1941. This type was a forerunner of the highly successful Fl 282, and was powered by a 140-hp (104-kW) Siemens Halske Sh 14a engine.

Helicopters of the World

mounted on drive shafts which are closely together and slope slightly outwards. The shafts are geared to the same main gearbox so that neither rotor can turn independently of its partner. Each blade always swings round exactly mid-way between two blades of the rotor on the opposite side. One of the advantages of this scheme is that the drive torque in the left shaft cancels out that in the right shaft, so no tail rotor is needed.

After intensive testing the neat single-seat Fl 265 was flown in May 1939. Early prototypes did well in tests with the Wehrmacht (German armed forces), and one survived a 20-minute dogfight with a Bf 109 and an Fw 190 without the camera guns of the fighters scoring a single 'hit'. This seemed to disprove the belief that helicopters could easily be shot down. In 1940 mass production was ordered, but the order was later transferred to a later design, the Fl 282 Kolibri (Humming Bird). The Fl 282 was able to carry an observer as well as the pilot, and in July 1940 work began on 30 prototypes and 15 pre-production machines. This was the first helicopter in the world to be built in numbers. By 1943 some 60 pilots had flown the 40 examples then completed, and 1,000 were on

This rare picture shows the first prototype Fa 223 Drache (Kite) on service trials with the Luftwaffe. It was the first of 30 development machines built at Bremen in 1940-2.

The Focke-Achgelis Fa 223 Drache was the world's first capable transport helicopter, originally planned as a civil machine for Lufthansa. Here in 1942 the second prototype, D-OCEW, is seen on acceptance trials.

Many Focke-Achgelis Fa 330s were captured after the war and were extensively tested by the Allies. The modern gyro-glider (used for gyrocopter training), which is usually towed behind a car, differs little in layout from this machine, which is currently displayed at RAF St Athan.

order by February 1944, but the programme was almost halted by Allied bombing of the factories. Several were used operationally both from ships and land bases, some having hair-raising adventures towards the close of the war.

Meanwhile the Focke-Achgelis company had gone on from the Fa 61 and designed the Fa 266 six-seat airliner for Deutsche Lufthansa. But in 1940 it was redesignated as the Fa 223 Drache (Kite) for military duties, and throughout World War II this was by far the most capable production helicopter in the world. It had a 1,000-hp (746-kW) engine driving the left and right rotors, and the capacious fuselage could house a pilot, observer, machine-gun in the nose, various bombs or mines, radio, radar altimeter, electric rescue hoist, and a sling for an external load of 2,822 lb (1280 kg) (or various loads could be carried internally). To show what this machine was capable of, one was sent to rescue 17 people trapped in the snow on Mont Blanc. The pilot was confident of bringing them all back at once, but sadly the machine crashed because of a fracture in a small forged link. Hundreds of the type were planned, but again Allied bombing wrecked the factories and not more than 35 were completed. French and Czech versions continued to be built in 1945-9.

The German Kriegsmarine in 1942-4 used large numbers of Focke-Achgelis Fa 330 Bachstelze rotor kites towed by surfaced U-boats to give long-range surveillance. This one is being tested in the giant wind tunnel at Chalais-Meudon, France, after the war.

For sheer numbers the top wartime rotorcraft was the simple Fa 330 rotor-kite, a form of autogyro glider which was mass-produced for use by U-boats. Each submarine could surface and bring the neat package on deck; in 10 minutes the Fa 330 would be unfolded, assembled, connected by a towing cable and its single rotor given a push to get it into the air. Thereafter the U-boat had a pair of eyes with powerful binoculars at a height of 400 ft (120 m), giving a view 25 miles out – five times as far as the horizon from the conning-tower. The Fa 330, called Bachstelze (Water Wagtail), was very useful, but several of the pilots were drowned when Allied aircraft approaching at high speed forced the U-boat commander to make a crash-dive, without waiting for his comrade aloft!

Thus the Germans were the first to make serious use of helicopters and other rotorcraft. In the

Helicopters of the World

The great Igor Sikorsky, managing to keep on his trilby hat despite the rotor downwash, attending the very first test of his VS-300 helicopter on the airfield at Stratford, Connecticut, on 14 September 1939. The unruly machine was chained to a heavy metal plate to prevent any catastrophic manoeuvres. It did not make a completely free flight until 13 May 1940.

Soviet Union more than 400 autogyros were built by 1946, some of them having fuselages (and engine/propeller units) similar to those of fighters and able to reach speeds up to 176 mph (283 km/h). Another design team under I. P. Bratukhin worked from 1938 on quite large helicopters having slim wings carrying an engine and rotor on each tip. By the end of the war the Bratukhin machines had engines of over 550 hp (410 kW), making them the world's most powerful helicopters. Most had a crew of three and were equipped either as ambulances or for artillery observation, the latter series having fully glazed noses with a large cupola above.

Igor Sikorsky

Today not many people remember Bratukhin, yet every student of the helicopter knows the name Sikorsky. After escaping from the Russian revolution Igor Sikorsky eventually settled in the USA, where he built famous amphibians and flying-boats. In 1938 he picked up the helicopter where he had left off in 1910, and he himself was at the controls when his VS-300 began its long and often frustrating programme of flight development on 14 September 1939. It began with a single main rotor and single tail rotor, and after more than two years ended the same way, but in between it was completely rebuilt 18 times to try and make it better! Sikorsky, at least as much as anyone else, found the helicopter a very difficult beast to tame. But on 6 May 1941 he broke the endurance record by staying in the air for more than 1 hour 32 minutes, and though one of the early US Army

Among other Soviet helicopter pioneers, I.P. Bratukhin was responsible for an important succession of large twin-engined machines with twin lateral rotors, which were originally influenced by the success of the Focke-Achgelis Fa 61 in 1938. This Bratukhin G-4 of 1945 demonstrates its hovering stability.

Probably taken during atom-bomb testing at Eniwetok in the Pacific in 1946, this shows one of the 100 production Sikorsky R-4B helicopters built for the USAAF. They closely resembled the YR-4Bs of 1943, but had a little more power – 200 hp (149 kW) instead of 180 hp (134 kW).

test pilots who flew it in that year said, 'More than anything else the VS-300 reminded me of a bucking bronco', it was the seed from which was to stem the world's first enduring helicopter company.

In 1941 Sikorsky's design team under Mike Gluhareff produced the proposed production machine, the VS-316A. It had an enclosed cabin at the front for two pilots side-by-side. Behind them was the 165-hp (123-kW) engine, driving the three-blade main and tail rotors. Construction was mainly of welded steel tube, with fabric covering. The VS-316A first flew on 14 January 1942. By 18 May the prototype had become the XR-4 of the Army Air Force, and on that date it left on a remarkable 761-mile (1225-km) flight made in several easy stages to the Army test centre at Wright Field in Ohio. By 1943 a service test batch of R-4 helicopters had been flown in severe places from Burma to Alaska, and by the US Coast Guard and Royal Navy. An order for 100 was then placed, and

A Sikorsky R-4B helicopter seen hovering over the apron at an air base at Tinian, Marianas Islands, in November 1945.

Helicopters of the World

More than twice as powerful as the Bell H-13 series, the Sikorsky H-5 (S-51) still carried only the same load: two stretcher casualties. In Korean operations, however, the stretcher was at least protected from wind buffet by being inside a streamlined pod, through which the 'medic' could keep watch on each patient. This is an H-5G.

R-4s went into wide wartime service, called HNS-1 by the Navy and Hoverfly I by Britain's RAF and Fleet Air Arm. As far as US helicopters are concerned the first emergency flight took place on 3 January 1944 when blood plasma was rushed by a Coast Guard R-4 to a badly burned crew aboard a US Navy destroyer near New York. The first use of a rescue hoist came when the crew of a barge were hoisted to safety on 29 November 1945.

In August 1943 Sikorsky flew the first XR-5, with a 450-hp (336-kW) engine and streamlined fuselage of stressed-skin construction. Some 300 were built, plus another 139 made under licence in England by Westland, which called this model the Dragonfly. In October 1943 Sikorsky brought out the R-6, with a rotor similar to that of the R-4 but improved in detail and driven by a 225-hp (168-kW) engine. This was a really good-looking machine, and on 2 March 1944 the prototype flew 387 miles (623-km) non-stop from Washington to Wright Field, clearing the 5,000-ft (1525-m) Allegheny mountains en route.

Bell joins the field

Back in 1942 other Americans were busy with helicopters, and the first to fly was the Model 30 built by existing aircraft company Bell Aircraft. It was completely funded by the company, and from its first flight in early 1943 this 160-hp (119-kW) two-seater showed that Bell's idea for a simpler form of rotor, with two blades stabilized by a bar arranged at 90° with weights on the ends, was basically sound. From the Model 30 came the Model 47, which at first looked almost like the long-awaited 'flying auto' with its four small wheels and comfortable interior. On 8 March 1946 the Model 47 received the first certificate for commercial operation ever awarded a helicopter. By the mid-1970s more than 6,000 Model 47s had been delivered in 60 versions by Bell and foreign licensees in Italy,

The work of the early production versions of Bell 47, notably the H-13E, as carriers of casualties in the Korean front line, is familiar to millions from the TV series MASH. Here is the real thing, probably photographed in 1953. To ease ground handling many H-13s had wheels added to the trunnions which appear as small lumps on the skids.

Japan and Britain. Useful load was improved from 200 lb (91 kg) to 1,200 lb (544 kg), and even today vast numbers of these machines clatter overhead around the world, famed from the TV series *MASH* and countless screenings of these lattice-tailed bubble-nosed machines in service with police, sheriff's offices and other operators from generals to crooks.

Bell moved on to the HSL-1, which was designed in 1950 to fly the challenging ASW (anti-submarine warfare) missions for the US Navy. This demanded the ability to operate from small platforms aboard quite modest warships whilst carrying ASW sonobuoys, a radar and torpedoes or depth charges. An autopilot, comprehensive radio and all-weather systems such as anti-icing were also mandatory. This was a far bigger job than any helicopter had been asked to do before, and it called for an engine of 2,400 hp (1790 kW), driving a rotor at each end of a slim but quite large fuselage. The HSL-1 could carry a useful load of 4,000 lb (1814 kg) of sensors and weapons, but the ASW mission proved too difficult to be fully accomplished and the 50 production machines spent most of their time as transports with 14 troop seats. But in 1956 Bell flew the first XH-40, a new machine for the US Army, and this led to the 'Huey' family, built in larger numbers than any other aircraft since 1945.

The helicopter comes of age

In Britain Bristol's team, led by Raoul Hafner, produced a competent small 4/5-seater called the Sycamore, but failed in prolonged attempts to build greatly stretched tandem-rotor machines (Types 173 and 191); they did develop a good ASW machine for the Royal Navy (the twin-turbine 192) but then had this cancelled and turned into the very unsuitable Belvedere transport for the RAF, which if it had been designed for the role from the start would have had a different arrangement. In the Soviet Union Yakovlev adopted the same tandem-rotor layout with the Yak-24 transport with two 1,700-hp (1268-kW) engines. A more successful exponent of the tandem-rotor configuration was Frank N. Piasecki, who flew his first (single-rotor) machine on 11 April 1943 and then in March 1945 flew his PV-3, popularly called 'The Flying Banana' because of its shape, lifted by a rotor at each end. This was built in quantity, and led to over 430 of the useful HUP Retriever family for the US Navy and Marines and to over 600 of the 1,425 hp (1063-kW) H-21 family, which were in production in 1956 when the company was renamed Vertol. From the extremely useful H-21 came the twin-turbine Model 107 passenger machine and its military variants the H-46 Sea Knight, still used today by the Navy and Marines, and of course the far bigger Chinook.

Sikorsky was careful not to jump ahead too fast and the R-4, 5 and 6 had all been basically two-seaters. In November 1949, however, the company flew the first S-55. This could carry a load of 2,800 lb (1270 kg), or 12 passengers, in a large cabin under the rotor carried on four small wheels. The engine, at first of 550 hp (410 kW), was in the nose inclined diagonally upward with the drive shaft passing up between the pilots, who sat right on top of the fuselage with their feet between the

Helicopters of the World

Large numbers of helicopters were used in Algeria, for the first time in attack and assault roles. The Armée de l'Air used hundreds of Sikorsky H-34s (S-58s), S-55s and Aérospatiale Alouettes, but the French army used these Piasecki (Vertol) H-21s.

cabin and engine. Sikorsky built no fewer than 1,281 of the military versions alone, and they did more work in the Korean war (1950-53) than any other helicopter. They were the first machines ever to bring back both pilots and aircraft shot down in enemy territory, artillery and ammunition to the front line, and rescue people in peril a dozen at a time. Westland built a series of improved versions named Whirlwind, culminating in versions with the Gnome turbine engine of over 1,000 hp (746 kW). A few of these are still in use as RAF and civilian rescue machines.

To follow the S-55 Sikorsky moved on to the S-58, flown in March 1954. Designed as the HSS-1 to do the US Navy ASW mission better than the HSL, it eventually matured not only in this role – which it did accomplish, unlike the HSL – but also in many transport versions seating 16 or 17 troops. The 1,525 hp (1138 kW) engine was again mounted in the nose, driving diagonally upwards as in the S-55, but the helicopter had a different appearance with a conventional rear fuselage instead of a slender tail boom, and a tailwheel and large rear fin (which could fold in the naval versions to fit into small ship hangars). As before the S-58 was licensed by Westland, and again the British company

With loaded side armament and a full complement of troops, a unit of Bell UH-1 assault transports prepares for lift-off and rapid transit to the designated landing zone.

The RAF used Westland Whirlwind HAR.Mk 10s for important rescue duties around the coast of Britain. These were replaced by Sea Kings.

transformed the US design with turbine power. Named Wessex, the British versions were powered either by the 1,450-hp (1082 kW) or 1,600-hp (1194 kW) Napier (later Rolls-Royce) Gazelle, or the Rolls-Royce Coupled Gnome with two 1,350-hp (1007-kW) turbines joined in one unit but giving twin-engine safety. Westland delivered some 360 of these fine machines to the RAF and Royal Navy, and they were visibly busy over the Falklands as they have been all over the world since 1957, mainly in the ASW and Commando assault roles, but also including The Queen's Flight.

In the Soviet Union the top helicopter design bureau soon emerged as that of Mikhail Mil, who has hardly had a single failure (except for the gigantic Mi-12 of 1968). Starting with autogyros, he moved on in 1947 to the neat Mi-1, followed by the 1,700-hp (1268-kW) Mi-4 of 1952, very much in the S-55 style but far more powerful and with seats for 18 passengers or various military loads (loaded through clamshell rear doors) or, in the Mi-14, a boat hull and ASW sensors and weapons. Some 5,000 of these fine machines were built, followed in 1957 by the gigantic Mi-6, by far the most capable helicopter of its day. Powered by two 5,500-hp (4103-kW) turbines driving a five-blade rotor of almost 115-ft (35-m) diameter, the Mi-6 was a real giant, yet it was also one of the fastest helicopters and in 1964 set a record at 211.4 mph (340 km/h). Able to lift a useful load of 44,350 lb (20120 kg), the Mi-6 first appeared laden with tanks and missiles, but in fact has been at least as useful in civilian roles, opening up Siberia and other underdeveloped regions of the Soviet Union. The Mi-10 and Mi-10K are special crane versions used for lifting and positioning very heavy loads.

Last of the important early helicopters, the French SNCASE (now Aérospatiale) Alouette (Lark) was also one of the smallest, being little bigger than a Bell 47 (or a Hiller 360 or UH-12, which in the 1950s gave Bell competition). The big difference with the Alouette II, flown on 12 March 1955, was that instead of having a droning, throbbing piston engine (heavy, and not only prone to failure but fuelled by high-octane petrol) it had a gently whistling turbine. This opened the way to more speed, more payload, smoother flight and improved safety. The Alouette II sold all over the world, to a total of 1,305 by 1975. This five-seater was soon followed by the seven-seat Alouette III, which has topped 1,450 examples!

In the frantically rapid preparation for the assault to recover the Falkland Islands, helicopters flew practically round the clock. One might say that everything that had to be moved was moved by helicopter, usually by a Commando (Westland Sea King HC.Mk 4). In this picture, however, the Sea Kings are ASW versions and the machine doing the trucking is a Westland Lynx of the Royal Navy.

A Westland Sea King Mk 43 of the Royal Norwegian air force practises air-sea rescue techniques off the Norwegian coast. Sea Kings also play a significant part in the important NATO task of shadowing the Soviet fleet (especially submarines) from their Arctic naval bases out into the Atlantic.

Naval Helicopters

The German navy used helicopters on warships in World War II, and the first Sikorsky R-4 just got in at the end of that conflict, but it was not until the 1950s that helicopters began to play a central role in almost all the tasks of a navy and an amphibious assault force.

The first Aérospatiale Super Frelons to go into service were the SA 321G version, used to support the comings and goings of the French nuclear-deterrent submarines by ensuring that they are not followed by hostile submarines. In this picture an SA 321G is seen launching an AM.39 Exocet anti-ship missile, during the latter's development.

The importance of the helicopter at sea is due to several factors. One obvious one is that the helicopter can go to sea aboard almost any surface warship, unlike the fixed-wing aeroplane. Another is that its unique flying capabilities fit the helicopter for a remarkably wide range of duties with a fleet at sea. Yet another is that the helicopter has a bracket of performance which fits it ideally to the increasingly difficult ASW task of finding and destroying submerged submarines. Since the mid-1950s the submarine has been able to dive much deeper than before and travel underwater at far higher speed, so that the task of destroying it has become very difficult for even the fastest surface ship (except the hydrofoil or air-cushion vehicle). Conversely, the fixed-wing aeroplane flies too fast to remain over its target and is reduced to making successive passes from a distance.

Helicopters of the World

It is thus not surprising that most of the pioneering uses of helicopters in war were at sea, with the German Flettner Fl 282 and American Sikorsky R-4. In 1944 the helicopter was a mere infant, and a very temperamental one. It could do little more than carry a pilot and observer (who, if he was not too big a man, could bring a pair of binoculars). In the previous chapter it was explained how difficult was the challenge faced by the pioneer Bell HSL-1, tasked with finding and destroying submarines. In the immediate post-war era even powerful ASW aeroplanes could not do the job alone: they were configured as either a hunter, laden with ASW sensors, or as a killer, with depth bombs or torpedoes. To do the job required a hunter/killer team of two aircraft, and the same was true of early ASW helos (which, with the somewhat dated word 'chopper', has become a common contraction for the unwieldy word helicopter). Thus the HO4S sub-series of S-55 helicopters of the US Navy (redesignated SH-19B from 1962) could carry either sensors or weapons but not both.

Anti-submarine warfare

Even the purpose-designed Sikorsky HSS-1 (S-58) proved to be incapable of doing an effective search and strike job, and at first this much larger and more powerful machine was used like the carrier-based aeroplanes in hunter/killer teams. By 1957, however, experience had shown that the HSS-1 could do a very good search job, being much faster and more agile than the parent ship or even the most nimble destroyer. Moreover, the technique of dipping sonar had been perfected: instead of having to drop its sensitive sonobuoys (which detect the submarine) into the ocean, the helicopter can carry just one and repeatedly dip or 'dunk' it into the water, listen for sounds of a submerged target, pull it up and move to a different place. As it need carry only one, or possibly one plus a spare, the sonobuoy can be much larger and more powerful or more sensitive than the expendable kind.

Thus the HSS-1 became a real extension to the eyes and ears of the ships. The helicopter searched and, when it found a target, it called up the surface ships to effect the kill. By 1957 the HSS-1N (after 1962 called the SH-34J) was in service, with all-weather and night gear including Doppler radar, autostabilization system and an auto-coupler to maintain the hover at a preset height, all of which meant better precision flying with reduced pilot workload. The British Westland Wessex HAS.Mk 1 was broadly similar, but the HAS.Mk 3 version had a more powerful engine which enabled it to do a better job, and in fact the Royal Navy Wessex has always been able to have a fair crack at performing the complete hunter/killer mission. The HAS.Mk 3 carries radar in a dorsal hump, resulting in its popular name of Camel, and it also carries up to two homing torpedoes plus sonobuoys.

One of the keys to the better performance of the Wessex, compared with the S-58, is its switch to turbine power. By the mid-1950s it was obvious that turboshaft engines were going to transform the helicopter very much for the better. Such engines are much lighter and more compact than piston engines of the same power, they are inherently far more reliable and they burn cheaper and generally much safer fuel. What was needed was a helicopter designed from the start for turbine power. Sikorsky's first to appear was the S-62, flown in May 1958. This quite small machine was actually lighter unladen than the S-55, but thanks to its new General Electric T58 engine it had almost double the power, could carry far more in a bigger cabin, and in addition it had a watertight boat-type hull and thus was amphibious. It was used mainly by the US Coast Guard.

The Sikorsky S-58, here seen in HUS-1 form with Navy squadron VX-6, was ideal for such utility tasks as distributing remote meteorological/radio stations to prearranged geographical positions in Antarctica. Later turbine-engined versions started more easily in extreme cold.

In the Falklands campaign the Westland Wessex did a great job with little publicity. Most were of the twin-engine HU.Mk 5 assault transport variety, but this is a Gazelle-powered HAS.Mk 3 'Camel' from No. 737 Sqn, normally operating from the destroyers Antrim *and* Glamorgan. *The former had a bomb pass under the pad without exploding, while the latter's hangar took an Exocet hit.*

What the US Navy wanted was a really effective ASW machine, and Sikorsky knew that by using two T58 engines they could build one. One of the new features of the S-62 had been that the T58 was so small and light (a mere 275 lb/125 kg) that it could be mounted above the cabin, next to the main rotor gearbox. This was how the bigger S-61 was designed, but with a pair of T58s side-by-side, with the air inlets facing ahead over the superb airline-style cockpit in the nose. Again the S-61 had an amphibious boat hull, with its twin main landing gears retracting into the side stabilizing floats. The first version was the HSS-2 (inevitably called the Hiss-2), the Navy ASW machine, first flown on 11 March 1959. After 1962 it was called the SH-3A, but its proud name did not alter: Sea King. Ever since it has been one of the world's leading helicopters in many fields, but its first task was ASW.

Lifted by a 62-ft (18.9-m) five-blade main rotor, driven by two T58s each rated at 1,250 hp (933

Distinctive in their brilliant yellow colour scheme, the Westland Sea King HAR.Mk 3 helicopters of the Royal Air Force are the latest SAR (search and rescue) machines for use around the UK's coasts and mountainous regions. Replacing the Whirlwind HAR.Mk 10, they entered service in early 1978, and the force of 16 were all in use the following year. All are nominally on the strength of No. 202 Sqn at Lossiemouth, Scotland, but are deployed in pairs at Boulmer (A Flight), Leconfield (B Flight), Coltishall (C Flight) and Lossiemouth (D Flight).

Westland Sea King and Commando

History and Notes
In the year the Sikorsky S-61 helicopter first flew (1959), Westland of the UK concluded a licence agreement, and the company developed the Sea King HAS.Mk 1 as the new ASW (anti-submarine warfare) helicopter of the Royal Navy, delivering 56 in 1969-72. Compared with the US Navy HSS-2 (SH-3), the Sea King HAS.Mk 1 has equipment for completely autonomous operation with no help from the parent warship, including dorsal radar, dunking sonar and a fully fitted tactical compartment for managing a whole ASW operation. These machines have been modified to Sea King HAS.Mk

2 standard with more powerful Rolls-Royce Gnome engines and improved equipment, 21 Sea King HAS.Mk 2 helicopters also being built new. The Sea King HAR.Mk 3 is the RAF SAR (search and rescue) model with very complete equipment and great versatility (SAR models carry up to 22 rescuees including stretcher casualties). The Sea King HC.Mk 4 is the RN (Marines) Commando, with the shipboard features (such as folding blades and tail) but simple fixed landing gear and fitted for 27 troops or 6,000 lb (2722 kg) of cargo. The Sea King HAS.Mk 5 is the current RN ASW model, with dramatically uprated avionics, all Sea King HAS.Mk 2s being converted to this

standard; 17 were built new and after the Falklands (when Sea Kings flew almost non-stop in terrible weather) nine more were ordered. Westland have exported ASW and SAR Sea Kings to eight countries and Commandos to various Middle East states.

Specification: Westland Sea King HAS.Mk 5
Origin: UK, based on US design
Type: ASW and multi-role helicopter
Armament: extremely comprehensive ASW sensors and systems plus up to four Mk 46 torpedoes or Mk 11 depth charges
Powerplant: two 1,660-shp (1238-ekW) Rolls-Royce Gnome H.1400-1 turboshafts
Performance: cruising speed at maximum weight 129 mph (208 km/h); range on standard fuel 764 miles (1230 km)

Weights: empty 13,672 lb (6201 kg); maximum take-off 21,000 lb (9525 kg)

Dimensions: main rotor diameter 62 ft 0 in (18.9 m); fuselage length 55 ft 9¾ in (17.01 m); height 16 ft 10 in (5.13 m); main rotor disc area 3,019.1 sq ft (280.5 m²)

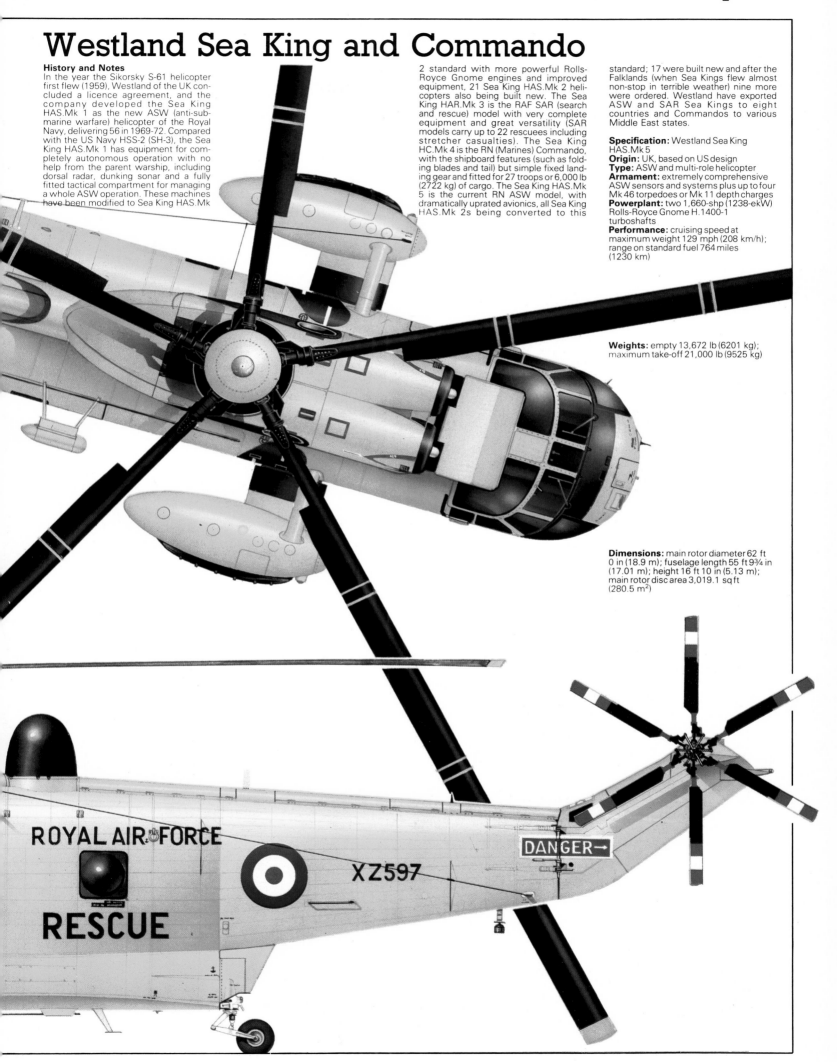

ROYAL AIR FORCE

RESCUE

DANGER→

XZ597

Westland Sea King HAS.Mk 5

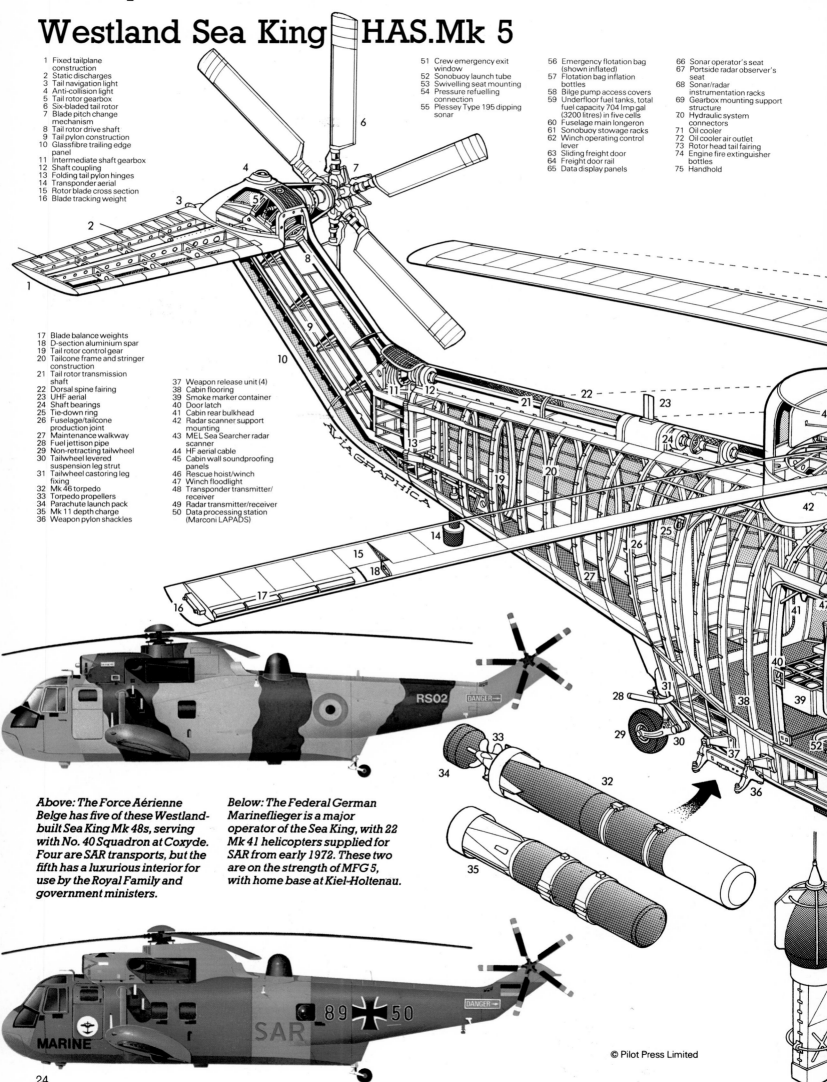

1 Fixed tailplane construction
2 Static discharges
3 Tail navigation light
4 Anti-collision light
5 Tail rotor gearbox
6 Six-bladed tail rotor
7 Blade pitch change mechanism
8 Tail rotor drive shaft
9 Tail pylon construction
10 Glassfibre trailing edge panel
11 Intermediate shaft gearbox
12 Shaft coupling
13 Folding tail pylon hinges
14 Transponder aerial
15 Rotor blade cross section
16 Blade tracking weight

17 Blade balance weights
18 D-section aluminium spar
19 Tail rotor control gear
20 Tailcone frame and stringer construction
21 Tail rotor transmission shaft
22 Dorsal spine fairing
23 UHF aerial
24 Shaft bearings
25 Tie-down ring
26 Fuselage/tailcone production joint
27 Maintenance walkway
28 Fuel jettison pipe
29 Non-retracting tailwheel
30 Tailwheel levered suspension leg strut
31 Tailwheel castoring leg fixing
32 Mk 46 torpedo
33 Torpedo propellers
34 Parachute launch pack
35 Mk 11 depth charge
36 Weapon pylon shackles

37 Weapon release unit (4)
38 Cabin flooring
39 Smoke marker container
40 Door latch
41 Cabin rear bulkhead
42 Radar scanner support mounting
43 MEL Sea Searcher radar scanner
44 HF aerial cable
45 Cabin wall soundproofing panels
46 Rescue hoist/winch
47 Winch floodlight
48 Transponder transmitter/ receiver
49 Radar transmitter/receiver
50 Data processing station (Marconi LAPADS)

51 Crew emergency exit window
52 Sonobuoy launch tube
53 Swivelling seat mounting
54 Pressure refuelling connection
55 Plessey Type 195 dipping sonar
56 Emergency flotation bag (shown inflated)
57 Flotation bag inflation bottles
58 Bilge pump access covers
59 Underfloor fuel tanks, total fuel capacity 704 Imp gal (3200 litres) in five cells
60 Fuselage main longeron
61 Sonobuoy stowage racks
62 Winch operating control lever
63 Sliding freight door
64 Freight door rail
65 Data display panels

66 Sonar operator's seat
67 Portside radar observer's seat
68 Sonar/radar instrumentation racks
69 Gearbox mounting support structure
70 Hydraulic system connectors
71 Oil cooler
72 Oil cooler air outlet
73 Rotor head tail fairing
74 Engine fire extinguisher bottles
75 Handhold

Above: The Force Aérienne Belge has five of these Westland-built Sea King Mk 48s, serving with No. 40 Squadron at Coxyde. Four are SAR transports, but the fifth has a luxurious interior for use by the Royal Family and government ministers.

Below: The Federal German Marineflieger is a major operator of the Sea King, with 22 Mk 41 helicopters supplied for SAR from early 1972. These two are on the strength of MFG 5, with home base at Kiel-Holtenau.

© Pilot Press Limited

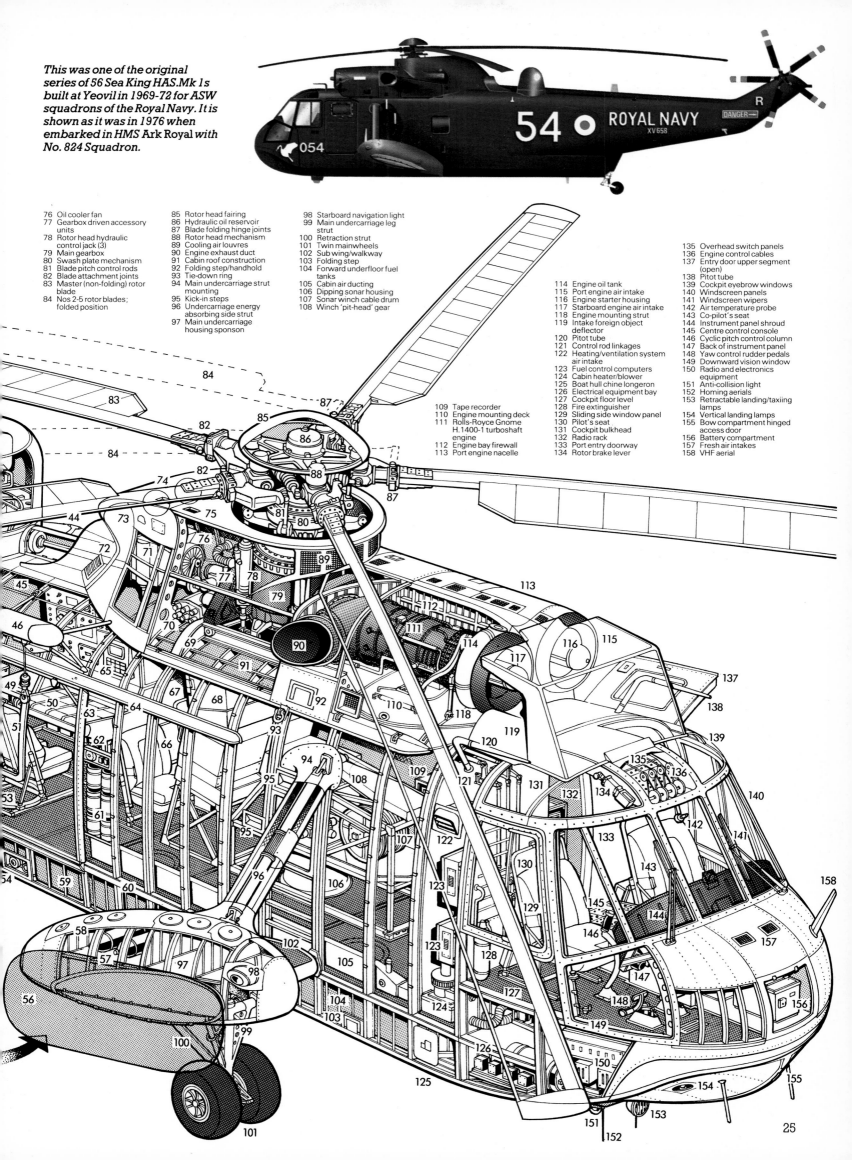

This was one of the original series of 56 Sea King HAS.Mk 1s built at Yeovil in 1969-72 for ASW squadrons of the Royal Navy. It is shown as it was in 1976 when embarked in HMS Ark Royal with No. 824 Squadron.

054   54   ⊙   ROYAL NAVY   R   DANGER →   XV658

76 Oil cooler fan
77 Gearbox driven accessory units
78 Rotor head hydraulic control jack (3)
79 Main gearbox
80 Swash plate mechanism
81 Blade pitch control rods
82 Blade attachment joints
83 Master (non-folding) rotor blade
84 Nos 2-5 rotor blades; folded position

85 Rotor head fairing
86 Hydraulic oil reservoir
87 Blade folding hinge joints
88 Rotor head mechanism
89 Cooling air louvres
90 Engine exhaust duct
91 Cabin roof construction
92 Folding step/handhold
93 Tie-down ring
94 Main undercarriage strut mounting
95 Kick-in steps
96 Undercarriage energy absorbing side strut
97 Main undercarriage housing sponson

98 Starboard navigation light
99 Main undercarriage leg strut
100 Retraction strut
101 Twin mainwheels
102 Sub wing/walkway
103 Folding step
104 Forward underfloor fuel tanks
105 Cabin air ducting
106 Dipping sonar housing
107 Sonar winch cable drum
108 Winch 'pit-head' gear

109 Tape recorder
110 Engine mounting deck
111 Rolls-Royce Gnome H.1400-1 turboshaft engine
112 Engine bay firewall
113 Port engine nacelle

114 Engine oil tank
115 Port engine air intake
116 Engine starter housing
117 Starboard engine air intake
118 Engine mounting strut
119 Intake foreign object deflector
120 Pitot tube
121 Control rod linkages
122 Heating/ventilation system air intake
123 Fuel control computers
124 Cabin heater/blower
125 Boat hull chine longeron
126 Electrical equipment bay
127 Cockpit floor level
128 Fire extinguisher
129 Sliding side window panel
130 Pilot's seat
131 Cockpit bulkhead
132 Radio rack
133 Port entry doorway
134 Rotor brake lever

135 Overhead switch panels
136 Engine control cables
137 Entry door upper segment (open)
138 Pitot tube
139 Cockpit eyebrow windows
140 Windscreen panels
141 Windscreen wipers
142 Air temperature probe
143 Co-pilot's seat
144 Instrument panel shroud
145 Centre control console
146 Cyclic pitch control column
147 Back of instrument panel
148 Yaw control rudder pedals
149 Downward vision window
150 Radio and electronics equipment
151 Anti-collision light
152 Homing aerials
153 Retractable landing/taxiing lamps
154 Vertical landing lamps
155 Bow compartment hinged access door
156 Battery compartment
157 Fresh air intakes
158 VHF aerial

25

Helicopters of the World

The Westland Sea King 50 is the standard ASW helicopter of the Royal Australian Navy's Fleet Air Arm Group serving with HS-817 squadron.

After the devastating Argentine air attack on the British landing ship Sir Galahad *at Bluff Cove, East Falkland in the 1982 Falklands conflict, a Royal Navy Sea King hovers over a liferaft. Many survivors were winched to safety during the operation.*

kw), the first ASW Sea Kings weighed about 12,000 lb (5443 kg) empty and could carry fuel for almost seven hours, and not only a full kit of ASW sensors but also 840 lb (381 kg) of ASW torpedoes, depth bombs or other weapons. To a considerable degree the old habits died hard, and the US Navy still used the HSS-2 (redesignated SH-3A after 1962) in partnership with the major surface combatant (ship) on which the helicopter was based. From the start the SH-3 family have gone to sea mainly in HS (ASW helo squadrons) units embarked aboard giant attack carriers as part of CVW (carrier air wings) operating alongside the fixed-wing ASW machines (at first the Grumman S-2 Tracker, later the Lockheed S-3 Viking). Many, however, are aboard dedicated ASW carriers, and a few serve aboard large frigates or cruisers, or at shore bases. With a gross weight up to 21,000 lb (9526 kg) and length with rotors turning of some 73 ft (22.25 m), the Sea King is not a machine for small ships.

ASW in operation

On the other hand, it was unquestionably the world's first helicopter with the full capability to fly the ASW search/attack mission unaided. Realization of its full potential in this role stemmed from the licence production of the Sea King by Westland in Britain, the first Sea King HAS.Mk 1 for the Royal Navy flying on 7 May 1969, some 18 months after the order for 56 of this type was placed. The Royal Navy required the main cabin, with four ASW operators, to be equipped as a self-contained tactical centre to manage a complete ASW operation. Though the autostab, Doppler, dorsal search radar, Plessey Type 195 dipping sonar, Newmark flight-control system, and such weapons as up to four Mk 46 torpedoes or four Mk 11 depth charges do not differ significantly (if at all) from those of the US Navy Sea King, the displays and management process were from the start tailored to completely independent operation. The system worked very well indeed, and was progressively improved in the more powerful HAS.Mk 2 version and now in the greatly updated HAS.Mk 5, to which all previous RN versions have been rebuilt. The HAS.Mk 5 has a visibly different radar and several new capabilities such as receivers for processing and displaying information from sensors unrelated to it, such as sonobuoys dropped by RAF Nimrods in a joint search. It is officially stated that the HAS.Mk 5 can 'pinpoint the position of an enemy submarine at far greater range than has been possible in the past' and then proceed to destroy it.

In the Falklands campaign Royal Navy Sea Kings of both Mk 2 and 5 varieties prevented a single submarine attack on the Task Force. They also performed such novel and frightening duties as presenting their broadsides to directions of possible attack to try to attract sea-skimming Exocet missiles and thus save surface ships from destruction; one HAS.Mk 5 flown on this duty was crewed by Sub-Lieutenant HRH Prince Andrew. Another duty, for which no aircraft was available, was that of airborne early warning. Just as the observer in the wartime Fa 330 rotor-kite could see much further than could his U-boat commander in the conning-tower, so can a surveillance radar 'see' further as it is raised above the earth's surface. The first AEW helicopters were two HR2S-1W (Sikorsky S-56 modified) of the US Navy of 1957. The S-56 was a very large transport helicopter used by the US Army and Marines, and it was the only VTOL machine of its day able to carry an APS-20E radar which gave it a giant distended 'chin'. In the South Atlantic in 1982 no such machines were available, and in 11 weeks two RN Sea Kings were converted to carry the Thorn/EMI Searchwater

Westland Sea Kings of the US Navy carried out all the recovery operations of Apollo astronauts from the ocean in 1969 and later. The task called for frogmen to be lowered to check the stabilized capsule, and a special cage to be used to hoist the three astronauts. On this occasion the helicopter was BuAer 152711, then an SH-3D and now an SH-3H, of HS-4.

Kaman SH-2 Seasprite

History and Notes
The original prototype HU-2K (later styled UH-2A) utility helicopter flew on 2 July 1959, and from 1962 Kaman delivered 190 of these very attractive machines each powered by a T58 engine and with fully retractable forward-mounted main landing gears. The UH-2A and UH-2B could each carry a 4,000-lb (1814-kg) slung load or 11 passengers, and did sterling work in planeguard, SAR, fleet reconnaissance, Vertrep (vertical replenishment) and utility transport duties, operating from many surface warships as well as at shore bases. From 1967 all available Seasprites have been converted to twin-T58 helicopters with full engine-out safety. Among many other models the most important current variant is the SH-2F (Mk 1 LAMPS, for Light Airborne Multi-Purpose System) for shipbased ASW and anti-ship missile defence with secondary SAR, observation and utility capability, in all weather. With a crew comprising pilot, co-pilot and sensor operator, the SH-2F can carry full ASW gear including surveillance radar, towed MAD bird, passive detection receiver, Difar and Dicass sonobuoys and comprehensive nav/com and display systems. The 4,000-lb (1814-kg) cargo ability remains, and a 600-lb (272-kg) rescue hoist is standard. From 1973 Kaman not only delivered conversions of earlier models but also 88 new SH-2Fs, followed in 1983-4 by 18 additional machines.

Specification: Kaman SH-2F
Origin: USA
Type: shipboard helicopter (see text)
Accommodation: three
Armament: one or two AS torpedoes (usually Mk 46)
Powerplant: two 1,350-shp (1007-ekW) General Electric T58-8F turboshafts

An SH-2F ordered as an HU2K-1U and later repeatedly rebuilt.

Performance: maximum speed 165 mph (265km/h); range with maximum internal fuel 422 miles (679 km)
Weights: empty 7,040 lb (3193 kg); maximum take-off 13,300 lb (6033 kg)
Dimensions: main rotor diameter 44 ft 0 in (13.41 m); fuselage length 40 ft 6 in (12.3 m); height 15 ft 6 in (4.72 m); main rotor disc area 1,521.0 sq ft (141.25 m²)

Kaman SH-2F Seasprite

Kaman Seasprite flying from USS Stanley over Soviet warships.

maritime surveillance radar in a giant 'kettledrum', normally projecting alongside the rear fuselage but in the search mode swung down through 90° to have a perfect view below the machine. Trials were eminently successful, and both helicopters joined the Task Force in August 1982. Five more AEW conversions followed.

So good was the basic S-61 Sea King that versions were produced under licence by Agusta in Italy and Mitsubishi in Japan. The Italian machines have been widely exported and include versions with large chin radar and a variety of locally developed weapon fits for the anti-ship role, including four wire-guided AS.12 missiles, two French AM.39 Exocet missiles or two of the Italian Sea Killer Mk 2 missiles in an integrated system known as Marte. In the USA the original SH-3A was several times improved in the 1960-72 period to the SH-3D standard with 1,400-hp (1044-kW) T58 engines and greater fuel capacity, the SH-3G utility transport and the SH-3H multirole Sea King with enhanced capability not only against submarines but also against sea-skimming missiles and in various EW (electronic warfare) roles.

For use from smaller ships the Kaman Corporation, located near Sikorsky in Connecticut, produced the SH-2 Seasprite. Kaman had been the chief US exponent of the Flettner 'eggbeater'

The neat and popular Kaman Seasprite has served for more than 20 years as a standard ship-based utility, rescue and ASW machine. This example was built as a single-engined UH-2B but later given two T58 engines to bring it up to UH-2C standard (the 1,250-hp/933-kW engines are limited to a combined power of 1,685 hp/1257 kW by the transmission, but either can safely fly the helicopter). It is shown rescuing a downed pilot, his position being made more evident by the release of fluorescent dye marker from his emergency kit.

Kamov Ka-25

History and Notes
Called 'Hormone' by NATO, this compact helicopter has appeared in various subtypes which have since 1965 been the standard type carried aboard Soviet surface warships. The traditional Kamov layout with superimposed coaxial rotors reduces disc diameter, and in any case automatic blade folding is provided for stowage in small hangars. Four-legged landing gear is specially tailored to operation from pitching decks, each leg having an optional quick-inflating flotation bag. The rear legs can be raised vertically, on their pivoted bracing struts, to lift the wheels out of the vision of the search radar always fitted under the nose. Two radars have been identified. The smaller type is carried by 'Hormone-A' on ASW missions, which also has a towed MAD bird, dipping sonar and electro-optical sensor (and possible others). A larger radar is fitted to 'Hormone-B' which is believed to be able to guide cruise missiles fired from friendly surface ships and, especially, submarines. Many other equipment items include a cylindrical container under the rear of the cabin and a streamlined pod under the tail. In 1982 Ka-25s were seen without flotation gear but with a long ventral box housing (it is believed) a long wire-guided torpedo. All Ka-25s have a large cabin normally provided with 12 folding seats additional to those for the crew of two pilots plus three systems operators. Some 460 of all variants were built by 1975.

Specification: Kamov Ka-25
Origin: USSR
Type: multi-role shipboard helicopter
Accommodation: flightcrew of two and three sensor operators, plus provision for 12 passengers
Armament: normally equipped with ventral bay or external box for two AS torpedoes, nuclear or conventional depth charges and other stores

Kamov Ka-25 'Hormone-C' multi-role SAR variant, with Yagi aerial above the radar.

Powerplant: two 990-shp (739-ekW) Glushenkov GTD-3BM turboshafts
Performance: maximum speed 130 mph (209 km/h); range with external tanks 405 miles (650km)
Weights: empty about 10,500 lb (4765 kg); maximum 16,500 lb (7500 kg)
Dimensions: main rotor diameter (both) 51 ft 8 in (15.74 m); fuselage length 32 ft 0 in (9.75 m); height 17 ft 7½ in (5.37 m); main rotor disc area (combined) 4,193.0 sq ft (389.7m²)

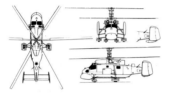

Kamov Ka-25 'Hormone'.

Kamov Ka-25 'Hormone C', with large chin radar.

layout after World War II, and in December 1951 flew the first helicopter in the world with a turboshaft engine. The final intermeshing-rotor series was the HH-43 Huskie rescue machine of the USAF and six other air forces. In 1959 the first Seasprite marked a switch to the conventional single main rotor, and with its T58 engine and retractable landing gear this looked a most attractive machine. From 1967 all Seasprites were rebuilt with two T58s in place of one, and from 1973 the standard model for shipboard use was the SH-2F. Still no larger than the compact earlier versions, this carries chin radar, sonar, a MAD (magnetic anomaly detector) device for finding submerged metal which distorts the Earth's magnetic field (also carried by most other modern ASW machines) and many other sensors or avionic units, as well as one or two torpedoes. The SH-2F, called LAMPS I (from Light Airborne Multi-Purpose System), is today deployed aboard all the latest US Navy frigates.

Three Kamov Ka-25 'Hormone' helicopters of the Soviet AVMF (naval air force) photographed from the walkway behind the funnel of the ASW carrier Moskva. The machine in the air is a 'Hormone-B' special electronics and missile-targeting platform, with bulged radar and no weapon bay. Those parked on deck are of the 'Hormone-A' anti-submarine type.

This colourful Aérospatiale SA 316C Alouette III is one of those used by France's Aéronavale (naval air force) for many kinds of mission. The only combat squadron is Flottille 34, based at Lanvéoc-Poulmic to provide helicopters singly or in pairs for service aboard warships in the ASW role. Others serve in SAR, communications and trials roles.

Powered by three 1,870-hp (1395-kW) Turmo engines, the large Aérospatiale SA 321G Super Frelon incorporates various Sikorsky features, not least of which is the basic technology of an amphibious hull. This version serves with Flottille 32 of the Aéronavale at Lanvéoc-Poulmic in the extreme tip of Brittany.

Its Soviet counterpart has for many years been the Kamov Ka-25, called 'Hormone' by NATO (which assigns invented names to all Soviet military aircraft). Like many earlier designs from this constructor, the Ka-25 has coaxial rotors which keeps down rotor diameter and results in a compact machine for naval use. Several versions are in service, with a large central cabin for the ASW or EW mission crew, and a chin radar, MAD, sonar and one or two torpedoes. Powered by two 900-hp (671-kW) turboshaft engines, these highly developed machines can carry a very wide range of mission devices, including EW electronics, special communications and systems for relaying to friendly warships (including submarines) exact positions of hostile targets beyond the horizon, and possibly for providing guidance information to naval cruise missiles in flight. In 1981 the new Ka-32 ('Helix') was first seen on the newly completed missile ship *Udaloy*; this has a more capacious cabin and many other changes, and with its ability to carry a cargo load of 11,023 lb (5000 kg) can be used

Helicopters of the World

Agusta-Bell AB.212ASW of the Marinavia (Italian naval air arm), which deploys 28 mainly aboard surface warships replacing the shorter and lower-powered AB 204AS. Note the dorsal radar and AS torpedo.

not only for Ka-25 duties but also for amphibious assault and vertrep (vertical replenishment, the bringing of supplies to surface vessels at sea).

There are many smaller naval helicopters, most of them unable to fly effective ASW missions but still sometimes deployed in that role. For example, the Italian Agusta company not only sold large numbers of AB 204, AB 205 and AB 212 helicopters (all licensed versions of the Bell 'Huey' family) to navies around the world but also designed the A 106 to fly ASW missions on a turboshaft engine of only 330 hp (246 kW). Indeed, Agusta even supplied ASW versions of the small piston-engined Bell 47 to the Italian navy, but as they could carry nothing but a pilot and a Mk 44 torpedo there was not much they could do except drop a torpedo at a place indicated by a surface warship. The otherwise popular Aérospatiale Alouette II and III have also gone to sea, but mainly in the observation and rescue roles.

Anglo-French contributions

Britain's smallest seagoing helicopter of recent years was the nimble Wasp, designed by Saro but produced by Westland using the Army Scout as a basis. Notable for its landing gear with four stalky legs with wheels specially arranged for use on a pitching deck, the Wasp has a 710-hp (530-kW) turbine and can carry six people, but is normally flown solo with two ASW torpedoes. Wasps became operational in 1963, and one of the last in RN service crippled an Argentine submarine off South Georgia in April 1982. A more modern light ASW helicopter is the versatile Hughes 500MD which does wonders on a mere 420 hp (313 kW) and is described in more detail in the next chapter.

Aérospatiale's biggest helicopter is the three-engined Super Frelon, and the first version to go into production was the SA 321G, delivered to the French Aéronavale from 1966. They have operated from the cruiser *Jeanne d'Arc*, but their routine task is to fly from the Ile Longue in support

Newest helicopter/missile combination in France is the Aérospatiale AS 332F Super Puma with two AM.39 Exocet missiles. The equipment fit includes nose weather radar and also a 360° Oméra ORB 3214 surveillance radar for targeting and to initiate missile guidance. Note the inverted slat on the sharply cambered tailplane.

Aérospatiale SA 365 Dauphin 2

History and Notes

Aérospatiale's single-engined SA 360 Dauphin and twin-engined SA 365 Dauphin 2 were developed to replace the Alouette III. First to fly was the SA 360 prototype, on 2 June 1972, powered by a 980-shp (731-kW) Turboméca Astazou XVI turboshaft. It was re-engined later with the 1,050-shp (783-kW) Astazou XVIIIA that now powers the production SA 360C Dauphin. On 24 January 1975 Aérospatiale flew the prototype of a twin-engined version of the SA 360C, the SA 365C Dauphin 2, powered by two 660-shp (492-kW) Turboméca Arriel 1A turboshafts. Its production has ended, but several versions of the Dauphin 2 are currently in production or under development.

These developments include the SA 365F to meet a Saudi Arabian requirement for a small helicopter that can operate from minor warships in search and rescue and anti-shipping roles. In the latter role the SA 365F will be equipped to carry four Aérospatiale AS.15TT anti-shipping missiles; first deliveries are planned for 1983. An SA 365M military version was under development in 1982 for general-purpose battlefield roles. The current production SA 365N commercial helicopter is similar to the original SA 365C, but has a high proportion of composites and carbonfibre in its structure. Final version is the SA 366 Dauphin 2 for service with the US Coast Guard under the designation HH-65A Dolphin.

Specification: Aérospatiale SA 365N Dauphin 2
Origin: France
Type: general-purpose commercial helicopter
Accommodation: flight crew of 1; up to 13 passengers
Powerplant: two 710-shp (529-kW) Turboméca Arriel 1C turboshafts

Aérospatiale HH-65A Dolphin SAR helicopter of the US Coast Guard.

Performance: maximum cruising speed 176 mph (283 km/h) at sea level; economic cruising speed 161 mph (259 km/h) at sea level; service ceiling 12,300 ft (3750 m); maximum range 548 miles (882 km)
Weights: empty equipped 4,398 lb (1995 kg); maximum take-off 8,488 lb (3850 kg)
Dimensions: main rotor diameter 39 ft 1¾ in (11.93 m); length, rotor turning 44 ft 2 in (13.46 m); height 13 ft 2 in (4.01 m); main rotor disc area 1,203.25 sq ft (111.78 m²)

Aérospatiale SA 360 Dauphin

Aérospatiale SA 365 Dauphin 2 carrying four AS.15TT missiles.

of the French fleet of ballistic-missile firing submarines, sweeping the sea ahead of any submarine going out on patrol to make sure it is not followed by a hostile submarine and tracked to its final patrol area. The Super Frelon was also one of the first aircraft to fire the Exocet heavy anti-ship missile, two of these powerful weapons being carried together with long-range Héraclès II radar. Exocet missiles can also be carried by the newer and more compact AS 332F Super Puma, while thanks to a giant order from Saudi Arabia the same company has also been able to develop the SA 365F Dauphin 2 in the naval role for ASW, rescue or in the anti-ship role with four of the new AS.15TT missiles. Earlier Aérospatiale missiles in this class had to be visually tracked and guided by operator commands passed along fine wires, but the AS.15TT is guided by the Agrion radar carried in the helicopter.

Britain's counterpart of the SA 365F/AS.15TT is the Lynx/Sea Skua, and both the helicopter and

A Boeing Vertol UH-46 Sea Knight ship-replenishment helicopter, from a special detachment aboard USS Camden (a fast combat support ship) nudges in towards the tiny aft platform of USS Wallace L. Lind, an elderly destroyer.

The Westland Lynx variant used by the French Aéronavale (naval air arm) differs from standard naval marks (of which there are 14) in having French equipment and weapons. The radar is the Oméra-Segid ORB-31-W, the dunking sonar is an Alcatel product, and weapons can include the Alcatel L4 torpedo and Aérospatiale AS.12 wire-guided missile (or, probably, the new AS.15TT). In this drawing the weapons are US-supplied Mk 44 torpedoes. Aérospatiale assists with production, one of its contributions being the main-rotor hub which is forged from a single slab of titanium.

Westland/Aérospatiale Lynx Mk 2

269 MARINE

DANGER →

269

History and Notes

Launched as part of the Anglo-French helicopter agreement of February 1967, this extremely modern and versatile machine is of wholly Westland design but production is shared 30 per cent by Aérospatiale, one of the French parts being the one-piece forged titanium hub for the four-blade semi-rigid main rotor. All versions have advanced digital flight control and all-weather avionics, and no previous helicopter equals the Lynx for agility and one-man all-weather operation. The Lynx AH.Mk 1 version is the British Army model with skid gear and eight TOW missiles plus roof sight (many other weapon options are possible). The Lynx HAS.Mk 2 is the baseline naval model with special shipboard wheeled landing gear, radar and comprehensive ASW (anti-submarine warfare) equipment or anti-ship missiles. The French Aéronavale model has Oméra radar, Alcatel sonar and AS.12 missiles. Many countries have bought naval Lynxes for ship ASW/anti-ship missions or coastal SAR (search and

rescue) with radar, hoist and accommodation for nine survivors. Almost 300 had been delivered of all marks by 1983, and new variants include the Lynx Mk 3 dedicated anti-armour helicopter with completely revised design for battle missions, and the large-bodied Westland 30 seating 22 troops or with 10 seats plus six stretchers (litters)

Specification: Westland Naval Lynx
Origin: UK/France
Type: shipboard ASW/anti-ship/SAR helicopter
Armament: two Mk 44 or 46 torpedoes or Mk 11 depth charges plus complete ASW sensor systems, or four Sea Skua or similar anti-ship missiles; many role kits and provision for 3,000-lb (1361-kg) slung cargo load
Powerplant: two 1,120-hp (836-kW) contingency rating Rolls-Royce Gem 41-1 turboshafts

Performance: cruising speed at maximum weight 140 mph (225 km/h) on either two engines or one; time on station at 58 miles (93 km) radius with full ASW sensors/weapons and all-weather reserves 2 hours 29 minutes
Weights: empty 6,680 lb (3030 kg); maximum take-off 10,500 lb (4763 kg)
Dimensions: main rotor diameter 42 ft 0 in (12.8 m); fuselage length 39 ft 1⅓ in (11.92 m); height 11 ft 9¾ in (3.6 m); main rotor disc area 1,385.4 sq ft (128.7 m²)

Westland/Aérospatiale Lynx HAS.Mk 2

Tailored exactly to the various shipboard roles, the Westland Lynx is the almost universal choice of the world's navies for use from surface warships. This early production HAS.Mk 2 of 1976 was later fitted with Sea Skua pylons.

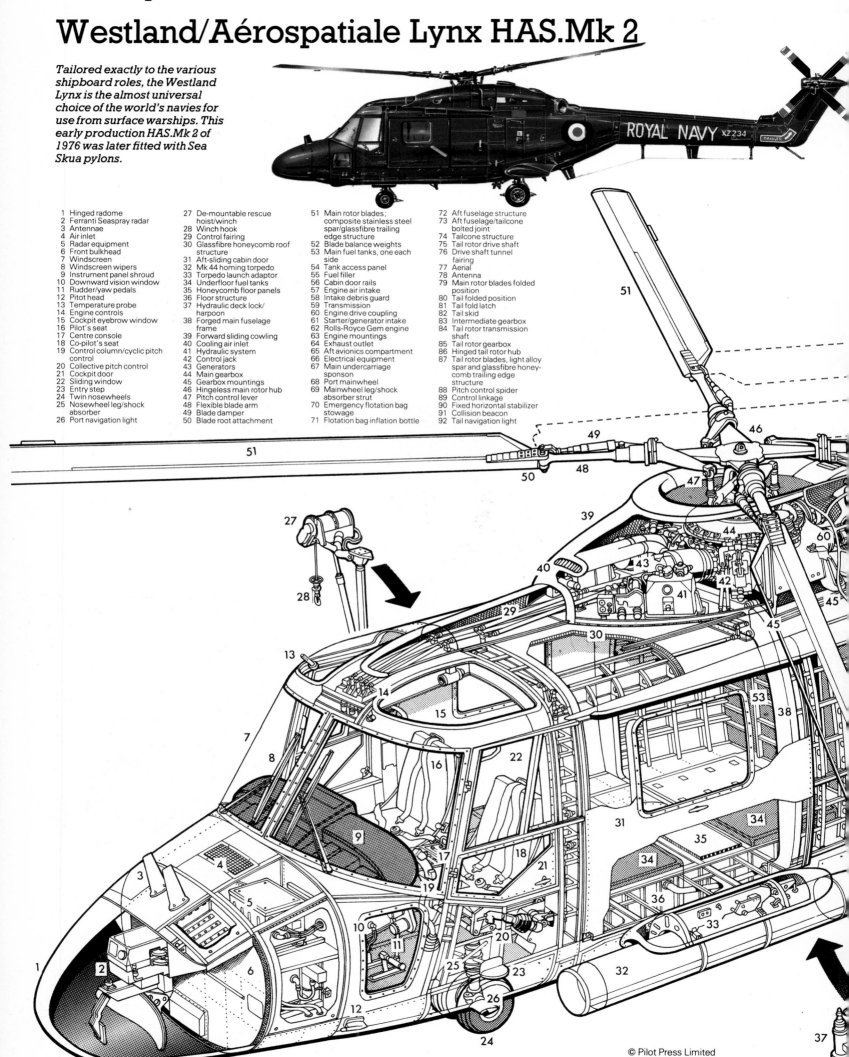

1 Hinged radome
2 Ferranti Seaspray radar
3 Antennae
4 Air inlet
5 Radar equipment
6 Front bulkhead
7 Windscreen
8 Windscreen wipers
9 Instrument panel shroud
10 Downward vision window
11 Rudder/yaw pedals
12 Pitot head
13 Temperature probe
14 Engine controls
15 Cockpit eyebrow window
16 Pilot's seat
17 Centre console
18 Co-pilot's seat
19 Control column/cyclic pitch control
20 Collective pitch control
21 Cockpit door
22 Sliding window
23 Entry step
24 Twin nosewheels
25 Nosewheel leg/shock absorber
26 Port navigation light

27 De-mountable rescue hoist/winch
28 Winch hook
29 Control fairing
30 Glassfibre honeycomb roof structure
31 Aft-sliding cabin door
32 Mk 44 homing torpedo
33 Torpedo launch adaptor
34 Underfloor fuel tanks
35 Honeycomb floor panels
36 Floor structure
37 Hydraulic deck lock/harpoon
38 Forged main fuselage frame
39 Forward sliding cowling
40 Cooling air inlet
41 Hydraulic system
42 Control jack
43 Generators
44 Main gearbox
45 Gearbox mountings
46 Hingeless main rotor hub
47 Pitch control lever
48 Flexible blade arm
49 Blade damper
50 Blade root attachment

51 Main rotor blades; composite stainless steel spar/glassfibre trailing edge structure
52 Blade balance weights
53 Main fuel tanks, one each side
54 Tank access panel
55 Fuel filler
56 Cabin door rails
57 Engine air intake
58 Intake debris guard
59 Transmission
60 Engine drive coupling
61 Starter/generator intake
62 Rolls-Royce Gem engine
63 Engine mountings
64 Exhaust outlet
65 Aft avionics compartment
66 Electrical equipment
67 Main undercarriage sponson
68 Port mainwheel
69 Mainwheel leg/shock absorber strut
70 Emergency flotation bag stowage
71 Flotation bag inflation bottle

72 Aft fuselage structure
73 Aft fuselage/tailcone bolted joint
74 Tailcone structure
75 Tail rotor drive shaft
76 Drive shaft tunnel fairing
77 Aerial
78 Antenna
79 Main rotor blades folded position
80 Tail folded position
81 Tail fold latch
82 Tail skid
83 Intermediate gearbox
84 Tail rotor transmission shaft
85 Tail rotor gearbox
86 Hinged tail rotor hub
87 Tail rotor blades, light alloy spar and glassfibre honeycomb trailing edge structure
88 Pitch control spider
89 Control linkage
90 Fixed horizontal stabilizer
91 Collision beacon
92 Tail navigation light

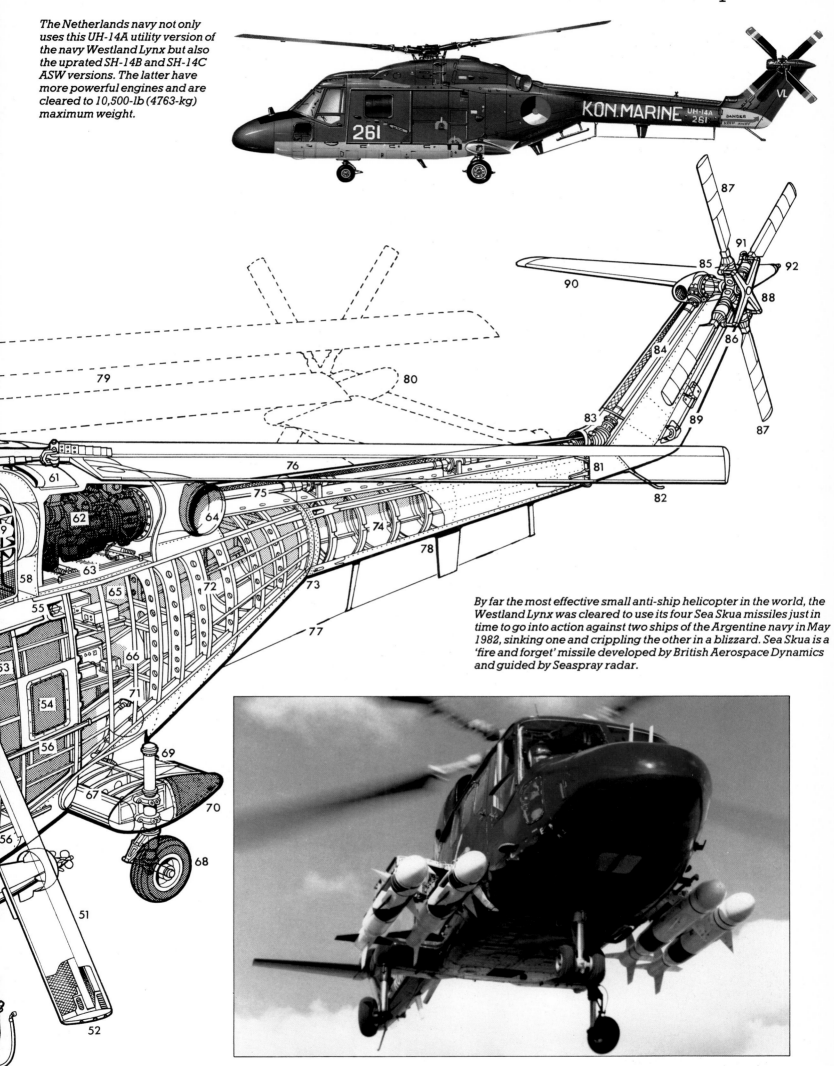

The Netherlands navy not only uses this UH-14A utility version of the navy Westland Lynx but also the uprated SH-14B and SH-14C ASW versions. The latter have more powerful engines and are cleared to 10,500-lb (4763-kg) maximum weight.

By far the most effective small anti-ship helicopter in the world, the Westland Lynx was cleared to use its four Sea Skua missiles just in time to go into action against two ships of the Argentine navy in May 1982, sinking one and crippling the other in a blizzard. Sea Skua is a 'fire and forget' missile developed by British Aerospace Dynamics and guided by Seaspray radar.

Helicopters of the World

Almost the only military aircraft supplied from Britain to Argentina in recent years have been two Westland Lynx Mk 23 to equip the two new Type 42 destroyers. Eight of the more advanced Mk 87s are on order.

the missile are more capable than the French types and exactly optimized for the naval missions. The Lynx is Britain's only modern helicopter, and it has already been produced in two distinct families for naval use and for army operations. Powered by two engines of from 750 hp (559 kW) to 1,120 hp (835 kW), the Lynx has a very advanced semi-rigid main rotor whose four blades are mounted in a hub forged from a slab of titanium (this component is one of those made by Aérospatiale under the terms of a 1967 agreement which assigned parts of the programme to France). This rotor and the ample power combine to make the Lynx possibly the world's most agile helicopter, with the ability to make sudden snap manoeuvres in all directions and also to perform repeated loops and rolls at high speed. In naval use the Lynx normally has a large search radar, and it can carry a full spectrum of ASW sensors and weapons, but most serve in the SAR (search and rescue) role with a high-speed winch and accommodation for nine survivors. Other tasks include anti-ship search and strike with four of the new Sea Skua missiles, which sank or disabled two Argentinian patrol vessels near the Falklands in extreme blizzard conditions in May 1982. Lynxes can also carry 10 troops, or loads up to 3,000 lb (1360 kg) in the vertrep role, and other duties include special communications, EW, reconnaissance and fire support.

Russian and American counterparts

Counterpart of the Lynx in the US Navy is the much larger and more costly Sikorsky SH-60B Seahawk. With rotors turning this has a length of 64 ft 10 in (20 m), compared with 49 ft 9 in (15 m) for the Lynx, and its engines are GE T700s of more than twice the power for lifting a helicopter weighing up to 21,884 lb (9926 kg) (more even than a Sea King). Equipment includes radar, MAD gear, sonobuoy tubes on the left side and up to two ASW torpedoes. It can also fly ASST (anti-ship surveillance and targeting) missions, though weapons in this role had not been announced in 1983 when deliveries of the SH-60B began.

It is remarkable that the Soviet Union has not yet revealed a really capable modern multi-role naval helicopter, though maybe the Ka-32 will develop into one. The Mi-14 is a large and powerful machine used in the ASW role, and possibly this can also fly anti-ship and SAR, missions but it has never been seen carrying missiles and it is not thought to be truly amphibious. It is related to the capable Mi-8 and Mi-17, which can seat up to 28 passengers but have not been seen in naval roles. Likewise the mass-produced family of Mi-24 helicopters bristle with sensors and weapons but none has any relevance to naval warfare.

Much larger and more costly than the Westland Lynx, the US Navy's Sikorsky SH-60B Seahawk has to carry an exceptional range of sensors, equipment and weapons. Most are armed with two anti-submarine torpedoes.

Not very much is known in the West about the AVMF's (Soviet naval air arm) shore-based ASW helicopter, the Mil Mi-14 'Haze'. Obviously closely related to the Mi-8 and also the Mi-24 assault helicopters, it has a watertight but not fully amphibious hull and the tricycle landing gear retracts to reduce drag and avoid unwanted interference with the large search radar under the nose.

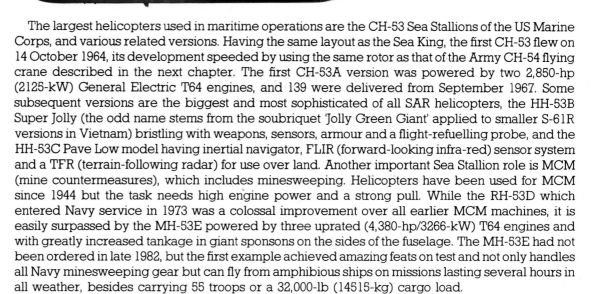

The largest helicopters used in maritime operations are the CH-53 Sea Stallions of the US Marine Corps, and various related versions. Having the same layout as the Sea King, the first CH-53 flew on 14 October 1964, its development speeded by using the same rotor as that of the Army CH-54 flying crane described in the next chapter. The first CH-53A version was powered by two 2,850-hp (2125-kW) General Electric T64 engines, and 139 were delivered from September 1967. Some subsequent versions are the biggest and most sophisticated of all SAR helicopters, the HH-53B Super Jolly (the odd name stems from the soubriquet 'Jolly Green Giant' applied to smaller S-61R versions in Vietnam) bristling with weapons, sensors, armour and a flight-refuelling probe, and the HH-53C Pave Low model having inertial navigator, FLIR (forward-looking infra-red) sensor system and a TFR (terrain-following radar) for use over land. Another important Sea Stallion role is MCM (mine countermeasures), which includes minesweeping. Helicopters have been used for MCM since 1944 but the task needs high engine power and a strong pull. While the RH-53D which entered Navy service in 1973 was a colossal improvement over all earlier MCM machines, it is easily surpassed by the MH-53E powered by three uprated (4,380-hp/3266-kW) T64 engines and with greatly increased tankage in giant sponsons on the sides of the fuselage. The MH-53E had not been ordered in late 1982, but the first example achieved amazing feats on test and not only handles all Navy minesweeping gear but can fly from amphibious ships on missions lasting several hours in all weather, besides carrying 55 troops or a 32,000-lb (14515-kg) cargo load.

One can almost sense the colossal threshing power transmitted by the seven-blade rotor of this Sikorsky CH-53E Super Stallion of the US Marine Corps, pictured over the Atlantic off Connecticut in 1981. This version has a much larger fin, inclined to the left complete with the tail rotor, the tailplane being gull-winged to bring the outboard portion horizontal.

Battlefield Helicopters

The first helicopters used in land battles in significant numbers were the front-line utility transports of the Korean war; then the French in Algeria used large numbers of armed helicopters. Today there are several quite distinct families of tactical helicopter.

The widely-exported Aérospatiale Puma is as powerful as a Sea King but much more compact. This example is seen with the SAAF over typical African jungle terrain.

Below: Bell Helicopter Textron and its foreign licensees have built more 'Huey' helicopters than any other single type of aircraft since World War II with the sole exception of the Antonov An-2 biplane transport.

Helicopters played little part in World War II, though it was the Germans' intention to use such machines as the Focke-Achgelis Fa 223 in large numbers to support their front-line troops and do many tactical duties. In Korea hundreds of helicopters flew mainly in the casevac (today called medevac, medical evacuation) role, while others brought supplies to the front line. On some occasions helicopters were used to reposition such equipment as mortars and light artillery, and to shuttle troops to different parts of the front line, but it was all on a small scale. Moreover the early helicopters were not equipped to fly in bad weather or at night.

A few helicopters were experimentally fitted with weapons, such as machine-guns or rocket launchers, but they had little practical effect. Nobody knew how best to use an armed helicopter and the machines were themselves highly vulnerable.

The Soviet Union flew the monster Mil Mi-6 in 1957, and immediately demonstrated it in highly tactical roles, in connection with large-scale army exercises. Tracked vehicles, large rockets and

Helicopters of the World

One of the 52 foreign military customers for the Aérospatiale SA 316C Alouette III is South Africa, which uses at least 40 and possibly as many as 70 for training, liaison, COIN assault and utility duties. Alouette III units are at Durban, Ysterplaat, Port Elizabeth, Bloemspruit and Zwartkop.

many other items weighing up to 12 tonnes were shown being unloaded through large rear doors, while as many as 90 personnel could be taken on board at once. This was far more than could be flown in Western machines, by far the largest of which was the Sikorsky S-56, designed for the US Marines in 1952 as the HR2S-1 but eventually used by the Marines and Army as the H-37 (Army name Mojave), able to load a Jeep or other loads up to 8,000 lb (3629 kg) or as many as 36 troops for short distances. The Marines had 55 and the Army 94, but these totals compare unfavourably with the 600-odd (out of over 800 built) Mi-6 giants that have served for 20 years with the Soviet tactical forces.

French determination

Until after 1960 most tactical helicopters were quite small. By far the most numerous were the small two/three-seat Bell, Hiller and Hughes piston-engined machines which for short distances could just manage a pair of stretcher casualties carried externally fixed to the landing skids. The French Aérospatiale SA 313 Alouette II of 1955 began the process of transformation to turbine power, but this again was a small machine, quite limited in range and speed, but because of its light and powerful engine able to seat two in front (one the pilot) plus three more passengers on a rear bench. The French did a great deal of pioneering with helicopters in land warfare, first in Indo-China in 1951-4 and from 1959 in the bitter struggle in Algeria. In Indo-China the French learned that the mobility of the helicopter could also be allied directly with firepower, by fitting guns up to 20-mm (0.5-in) calibre, rockets and even bombs, in addition to using helicopters to bring in supplies and take out casualties. But helicopters were low-powered and in short supply in that depressing conflict, and when it came to the struggle for Algeria the French were determined to do better. They scoured the world for the most powerful helicopters they could get, and not only imported hundreds of Vertol H-21 Shawnee transports but also 90 S-58s from Sikorsky, as well as building a further 166 S-58s under licence. Called Eléphant Joyeux (Happy Elephant), the S-58s not only carried troops and weapons but were themselves fitted with greater firepower than any previous helicopters. One of the new weapons was the wire-guided missile, steered exactly to its destination by electrical signals from an operator in the helicopter looking at the target through a magnifying sight. Intended for use against tanks, these SS.10 and SS.11 missiles proved devastating when used against Algerians semi-hidden in buildings or mountains. The French were still driven

One of the largest operators of the Aérospatiale SA 313 Alouette II is still the ALAT (French army light aviation), which still has many in Groupes d'Hélicoptères Légères attached to each army division, operating alongside Alouette IIIs (some with AS.11 missiles), Gazelles (many with HOT missiles) and Pumas. Alouette IIs have been replaced in observation and light transport roles by Gazelles, but still serve for training and light utility duties.

A standard Aérospatiale SA 330H Puma serving with the Force Aérienne Belge, five being used by No. 15 Squadron at Brasschaat alongside three operated by the Gendarmerie Nationale. They are painted for high contrast against the ground all the year round.

Complementing the light tactical Agusta-Bells, the standard transport helicopter of the Royal Moroccan air force is the Aérospatiale SA 330, a total of 40 having been supplied. They have been heavily engaged in operations against Polisario guerrillas.

from Algeria, however; and even more surprising is the fact that Algeria is a good market for French armaments!

One of the French products bought by Algeria is the Aérospatiale Puma helicopter. This was designed in 1962-4 at the height of the Algerian war, and it was based on the experience gained in that conflict. The ALAT (French army light aviation) had a clear need for a modern helicopter in the style of the Sea King, much better than the piston-engined H-21 and S-58, and equipped with a large cabin with a level floor close to the ground and with equipment for all-weather flying by day or night. Called a *hélicoptère de manoeuvre*, the new machine was needed to fly all army tactical roles, in all climates. It was designed very much like the Westland Sea King but more compact and without amphibious capability. Despite the use of two 1,575 hp (1174-kW) engines (more power than most Sea Kings), the Puma has a four-blade main rotor of only 49-ft (15-m) diameter, and its maximum weight of 16,315 lb (7400 kg) is much lighter. Thus the Puma has a high performance and good manoeuvrability. The standard machine has retractable twin-wheel tricycle landing gear, but one prototype was built with 'high flotation' gears able to traverse soft muddy areas, sand or even snow, and with a power drive so that the helicopter can taxi on the ground (for example, to get under prepared camouflaged hides without the rotors running).

Almost 700 Pumas have been built, most of them for armies and air forces, and including some assembled in Britain for the RAF and a larger number built under licence in Indonesia. Though normally used as an assault transport with 20 troops, Pumas have carried a range of weapon fits including cannon, machine-guns, wire-guided missiles and rockets, and options include weather

Aérospatiale SA 330B Pumas of the French ALAT (army light aviation) with landing gear extended. These capable machines are used for general transport in battle areas, medevac combined with forward-area resupply, and such special duties as emplacement of Milan anti-tank missile teams.

Aérospatiale SA 330 Puma

History and Notes
The SA 330 Puma was developed by Aérospatiale (then Sud-Aviation) to meet a French army need for an all-weather medium transport helicopter. In 1967 it was also selected for the RAF and produced as a joint programme with Westland. Features of the SA 330 include stressed-skin construction, a fully articulated four-blade main rotor driven by two engines immediately ahead of the hub, a large unobstructed cabin with a jettisonable sliding door on each side, fuel in tanks under the cabin floor, and tricycle landing gear with all units fully retractable, the twin-wheel main gears folding into side sponsons. Nearly 700 Pumas were built for at least 25 air forces, the SA 330L having glassfibre rotor blades and increased load and performance. In 1978 the first AS 332 led to today's Super Puma with 1,780-shp (1328-ekW) Makila engines driving an advanced rotor system, with complete all-weather protection and avionics, longer nose, new single-wheel main gears and a new tail. The main military models are the AS 332B 20-seater, AS 332F naval version for ASW/SAR/anti-ship missions, and the AS 332M with stretched fuselage seating 24.

Specification: Aérospatiale SA 330L
Origin: France
Type: utility transport helicopter
Accommodation: numerous schemes for up to 20 passengers or cargo load up to 7,055 lb (3200 kg) on internally mounted sling
Armament: numerous options include machine-guns, cannon, rockets and wire-guided missiles
Powerplant: two 1,575-shp (1175-kW) Turboméca Turmo IVC turboshafts
Performance: maximum speed 163 mph (263 km/h) at maximum weight; cruising speed 160 mph (258 km/h); range without reserve 341 miles (550 km)
Weights: empty 7,970 lb (3615 kg); maximum take-off 16,535 lb (7500 kg)
Dimensions: main rotor diameter 49 ft 2½ in (15.0 m); fuselage length 46 ft 1½ in (14.06 m); height over tail rotor 16 ft 10½ in (5.14 m); main rotor disc area 1,905 sq ft (177.0 m²)

The Aérospatiale SA 330 Puma was designed to meet the needs of France's ALAT for an all-weather tactical airlifter. The basic force comprises 133 of the original model, two squadrons of which serve in each of the six Régiments d'Hélicoptères de Combat. Large numbers of Pumas were also supplied to l'Armée de l'Air, and an aircraft of ETAG 38 (serving overseas at Pointe-à-Pitre) is depicted.

58 MK

1515

DANGER

Aérospatiale AS 332 Super Puma

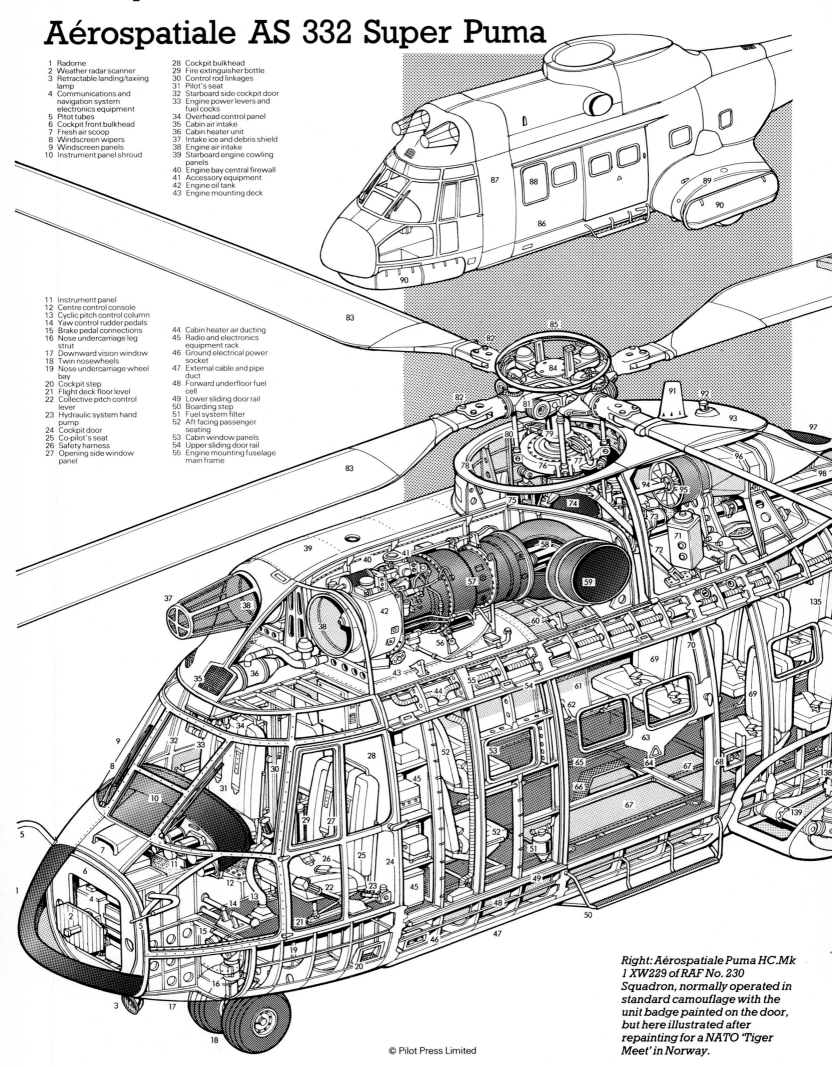

1 Radome
2 Weather radar scanner
3 Retractable landing/taxiing lamp
4 Communications and navigation system electronics equipment
5 Pitot tubes
6 Cockpit front bulkhead
7 Fresh air scoop
8 Windscreen wipers
9 Windscreen panels
10 Instrument panel shroud

28 Cockpit bulkhead
29 Fire extinguisher bottle
30 Control rod linkages
31 Pilot's seat
32 Starboard side cockpit door
33 Engine power levers and fuel cocks
34 Overhead control panel
35 Cabin air intake
36 Cabin heater unit
37 Intake ice and debris shield
38 Engine air intake
39 Starboard engine cowling panels
40 Engine bay central firewall
41 Accessory equipment
42 Engine oil tank
43 Engine mounting deck

11 Instrument panel
12 Centre control console
13 Cyclic pitch control column
14 Yaw control rudder pedals
15 Brake pedal connections
16 Nose undercarriage leg strut
17 Downward vision window
18 Twin nosewheels
19 Nose undercarriage wheel bay
20 Cockpit step
21 Flight deck floor level
22 Collective pitch control lever
23 Hydraulic system hand pump
24 Cockpit door
25 Co-pilot's seat
26 Safety harness
27 Opening side window panel

44 Cabin heater air ducting
45 Radio and electronics equipment rack
46 Ground electrical power socket
47 External cable and pipe duct
48 Forward underfloor fuel cell
49 Lower sliding door rail
50 Boarding step
51 Fuel system filter
52 Aft facing passenger seating
53 Cabin window panels
54 Upper sliding door rail
55 Engine mounting fuselage main frame

Right: Aérospatiale Puma HC.Mk 1 XW229 of RAF No. 230 Squadron, normally operated in standard camouflage with the unit badge painted on the door, but here illustrated after repainting for a NATO 'Tiger Meet' in Norway.

© Pilot Press Limited

Battlefield Helicopters

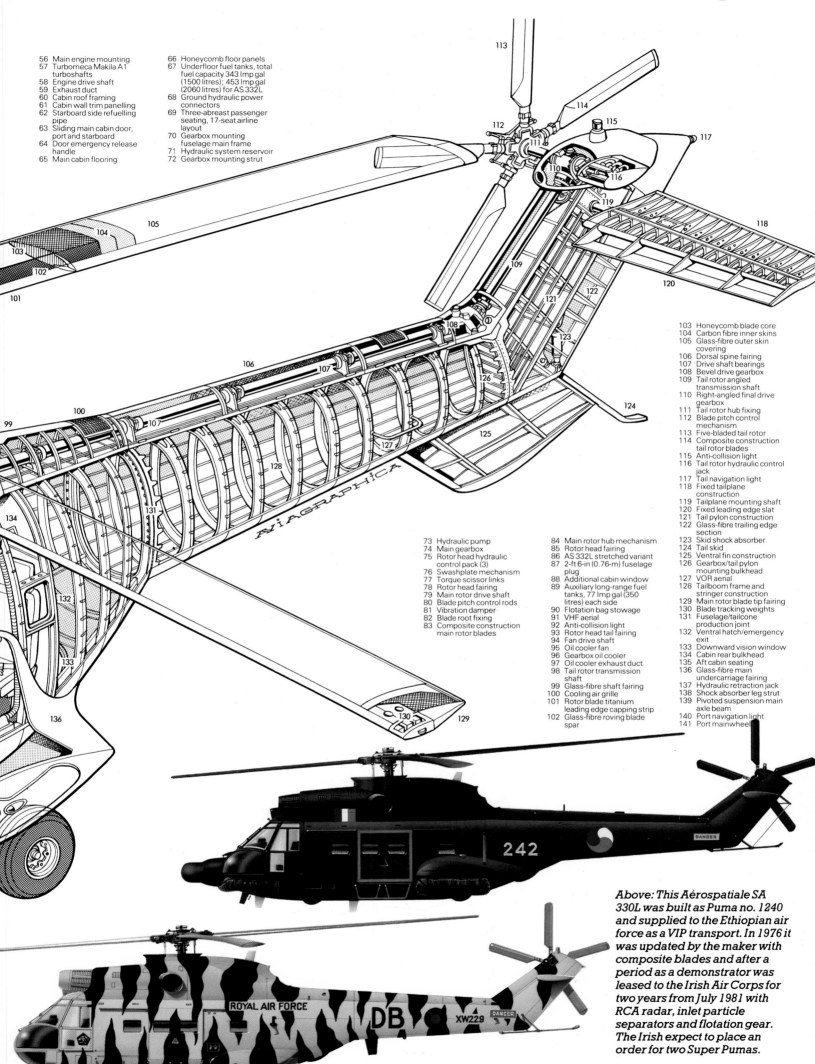

56 Main engine mounting
57 Turbomeca Makila A1 turboshafts
58 Engine drive shaft
59 Exhaust duct
60 Cabin roof framing
61 Cabin wall trim panelling
62 Starboard side refuelling pipe
63 Sliding main cabin door, port and starboard
64 Door emergency release handle
65 Main cabin flooring
66 Honeycomb floor panels
67 Underfloor fuel tanks, total fuel capacity 343 Imp gal (1500 litres); 453 Imp gal (2060 litres) for AS 332L
68 Ground hydraulic power connectors
69 Three-abreast passenger seating, 17-seat airline layout
70 Gearbox mounting fuselage main frame
71 Hydraulic system reservoir
72 Gearbox mounting strut

73 Hydraulic pump
74 Main gearbox
75 Rotor head hydraulic control pack (3)
76 Swashplate mechanism
77 Torque scissor links
78 Rotor head fairing
79 Main rotor drive shaft
80 Blade pitch control rods
81 Vibration damper
82 Blade root fixing
83 Composite construction main rotor blades
84 Main rotor hub mechanism
85 Rotor head fairing
86 AS 332L stretched variant
87 2-ft 6-in (0.76-m) fuselage plug
88 Additional cabin window
89 Auxiliary long-range fuel tanks, 77 Imp gal (350 litres) each side
90 Flotation bag stowage
91 VHF aerial
92 Anti-collision light
93 Rotor head tail fairing
94 Fan drive shaft
95 Oil cooler fan
96 Gearbox oil cooler
97 Oil cooler exhaust duct
98 Tail rotor transmission shaft
99 Glass-fibre shaft fairing
100 Cooling air grille
101 Rotor blade titanium leading edge capping strip
102 Glass-fibre roving blade spar

103 Honeycomb blade core
104 Carbon fibre inner skins
105 Glass-fibre outer skin covering
106 Dorsal spine fairing
107 Drive shaft bearings
108 Bevel drive gearbox
109 Tail rotor angled transmission shaft
110 Right-angled final drive gearbox
111 Tail rotor hub fixing
112 Blade pitch control mechanism
113 Five-bladed tail rotor
114 Composite construction tail rotor blades
115 Anti-collision light
116 Tail rotor hydraulic control jack
117 Tail navigation light
118 Fixed tailplane construction
119 Tailplane mounting shaft
120 Fixed leading edge slat
121 Tail pylon construction
122 Glass-fibre trailing edge section
123 Skid shock absorber
124 Tail skid
125 Ventral fin construction
126 Gearbox/tail pylon mounting bulkhead
127 VOR aerial
128 Tailboom frame and stringer construction
129 Main rotor blade tip fairing
130 Blade tracking weights
131 Fuselage/tailcone production joint
132 Ventral hatch/emergency exit
133 Downward vision window
134 Cabin rear bulkhead
135 Aft cabin seating
136 Glass-fibre main undercarriage fairing
137 Hydraulic retraction jack
138 Shock absorber leg strut
139 Pivoted suspension main axle beam
140 Port navigation light
141 Port mainwheel

Above: This Aérospatiale SA 330L was built as Puma no. 1240 and supplied to the Ethiopian air force as a VIP transport. In 1976 it was updated by the maker with composite blades and after a period as a demonstrator was leased to the Irish Air Corps for two years from July 1981 with RCA radar, inlet particle separators and flotation gear. The Irish expect to place an order for two Super Pumas.

Helicopters of the World

Like 60 air forces around the world, that of Morocco has standardized on the Huey family as utility transport helicopter. Agusta supplied 35 of these AB.205s, later followed by an initial five twin-engined AB.212s.

radar, rotor-blade thermal de-icing and special inlet attachments which prevent the ingestion of sand or sea spray. Since 1981 Aérospatiale has been delivering the more powerful AS 332 Super Puma, which has even higher performance and new equipment as well as better protection against hostile fire.

The Sikorsky S-61 itself was not used in the tactical land role, though the specially developed S-61R, with tricycle landing gear and a large rear ramp door, was important in Vietnam as the 'Jolly Green Giant' (HH-3E) rescue helicopter with armour, flight-refuelling probe, special navigation and communications systems, self-sealing tanks, rescue hoist and various weapons. The earlier S-55 and S-58 were, however, used in large numbers, though chiefly as plain front-line transports.

Far more important is Bell's so-called Huey family, the name stemming from the designation HU-1, which supplanted the original US Army H-40 designation but itself was changed in 1962 to UH-1. The XH-40 prototype was flown in October 1956 as a neat and modern turbine helicopter for the US Army to undertake all forms of tactical transport airlift duty but on quite a modest scale. The prototype had a T53 engine of 700 hp (522 kW) and was cleared to a gross weight of 5,800 lb (2631 kg). The engine, like other turbines, was compact and light enough to be tucked away above the cabin roof immediately behind the main rotor gearbox, so the cabin could be placed directly under the rotor with a smooth level floor and no obstructions, accessed by large sliding doors on either side leaving an open space through which the six occupants could leap as one man. The pilot and second crewman sat side-by-side in the nose with direct access to the cabin, unlike the S-55 and S-58 series where they were at an upper level.

One of the duties of various Bell UH-1 Iroquois ('Huey') helicopters during the Vietnam War was riverine patrol with weapons for use against the Viet Cong. Standard armament system was the M21, comprising two M134 six-barrel 7.62-mm (0.3-in) Miniguns, each firing at up to 4,000 rounds per minute, and two seven-barrel launchers for 2.75-in (70-mm) folding-fin rockets. The guns could be aimed through an angle of 82° and depressed to −85°.

Bell 204 and 205 HU-1 Iroquois

History and Notes
When Bell Aircraft (now Bell Helicopter Textron) won the contract in 1956 to build a prototype utility helicopter for the US Army, it little thought its successors would outnumber all other military aircraft since World War II. The original XH-40 had a two-blade rotor with stabilizer bar, rear elevator, skid gear, 700-hp (522-kW) T53 engine and accommodation for two pilots and six troops or two stretchers. Engine power grew to 960 hp (716 kW) and then to 1,100 hp (821 kW), and among numerous versions were USAF models with T58 engines and variants made by Agusta (Italy), some with Rolls-Royce Gnome engines) and Fuji (Japan). The Model 205, flown in 1961, introduced 1,400-hp (1044-kW) T53, longer cabin seating 14 troops or with space for six stretchers or a 4,000-lb (1814-kg) load, and among the numerous mass-produced versions were licensed types made by Agusta (AB.205), Dornier (West Germany), Fuji and AIDC (Taiwan). The latest Model 205 version is the US Army UH-1H, of which some 1,350 had been built by 1983. Recent efforts have centred on the EH-1H ECM version with complex emitter location, analysis and jamming systems, and the SOTAS (Stand-Off Target Acquisition System) variant with a giant rotating radar aerial under the fuselage.

Specification: Bell UH-1H
Origin: USA
Type: multi-role helicopter
Accommodation: pilot plus 11 to 14 armed troops, or 3,880 lb (1759 kg) of internal cargo, or six stretchers and attendant; related models have numerous role fits including weapons or ASW gear
Armament: see above
Powerplant: one 1,400-shp (1044-ekW) Avco Lycoming T53-13 turboshaft

Agusta-Bell AB 204B of the Austrian Luftstreitkräfte's Hubschraubergruppe 3 (3rd Helicopter Wing) based at Linz in the 1970s.

Performance: maximum speed (also cruising speed) 127 mph (204 km/h); range with maximum fuel and no allowances at sea level 318 miles (511 km)
Weights: empty equipped 5,210 lb (2363 kg); maximum take-off 9,500 lb (4309 kg)
Dimensions: main rotor diameter 48 ft 0 in (14.63 m); fuselage length 41 ft 10¾ in (12.77 m); height over tail rotor 14 ft 5½ in (4.41 m); main rotor disc area 1,809.6 sq ft (168.1 m²)

Bell UH-1B (204) Iroquois

Prototype Bell UH-1L Huey during a test flight.

From the start the manufacturers strove to improve a product that was already assured of large orders, initially from the US Army. The task was made easier by Avco Lycoming's continual uprating of the T53 engine, first to 860 hp (641 kW), then to 960 hp (716 kW), then to 1,100 hp (820 kW) and in the 1960s to 1,400 hp (1044 kW). This enabled the six-seat UH-1A to be 'stretched' into the 12-seat UH-1D (there were many other versions), with gross weight raised to 9,500 lb (4309 kg) and cargo load increased from 1,300 lb (590 kg) to 2,200 lb (998 kg), then to 3,300 lb (1497 kg) and in the UH-1D to 4,000 lb (1814 kg). Thousands of these, called Model 204 to 205 in civil or export forms, were built by 1970 and they far outnumbered all other US aircraft in Vietnam, where different models flew with the US Army (largest user), Air Force, Navy and Marine Corps. They were the standard assault helicopter for air cavalry and all other Allied airmobile forces, and many also served in rescue and other roles. Dornier made 352 in West Germany and another 118 were licence-built in Taiwan, all for military use.

Bell success story

The final Model 205 single-engine variant for US forces was the UH-1H of 1967, which can seat 14 troops and is today the most numerous helicopter in any Western service. The US Army plans to retain over 2,700 in front-line duty to beyond the year 2000, and is at present organizing delivery of 6,000 main-rotor blades made of advanced plastic composite materials, as well as a complete upgrading of the avionics and special warfare systems such as ECM, infra-red suppressed exhausts and flares to decoy IR missiles, special communications usable when flying at only just above the ground, and equipment for flight at night and in the worst weather. In 1968 Bell began producing the 212 (Two-Twelve) with the PT6T twin-engined powerplant having two power sections to give twin-engine safety. This model is used in numbers by the Marines, Navy and Air Force in utility,

Although this machine is not so equipped, 60 of the British army Westland Lynx AH.Mk 1 multi-role helicopters are armed with quad TOW missiles, with reloads in the cabin. Another task is to carry anti-tank infantry teams armed with the Milan missile.

assault and rescue roles. Other Hueys fly with large surveillance radars and special communications or other electronic gear, while the same basic design has now been stretched in the Model 214ST to capability undreamed of in the original 5,800 lb (2631 kg) machine, the two 1,635-hp (1219-kW) engines lifting a gross weight of 17,500 lb (7938 kg) and a streamlined fuselage seating 20, or with a cargo load of 8,000 lb (3629 kg) – half as much again as the gross laden weight of the Huey prototype!

Altogether Bell has built more than 15,000 Hueys, outnumbering all other types of aircraft since 1945 except the Soviet Union's Antonov An-2 biplane transport. The company has also built several thousand military versions of the small Model 206, powered by the Allison 250 (T63) turboshaft of 250 hp (186 kW) to 420 hp (313 kW). The first version was the OH-4A LOH (light observation helo) but this was beaten by the Hughes OH-6A, as related later. In 1968 the US Army reopened the LOW competition and awarded contracts to Bell for no fewer than 2,200 of an improved model designated OH-58A Kiowa, a utility and observation machine seating up to five (in the 206L LongRanger seven can be accommodated). From 1978 Bell rebuilt 275 Kiowas as OH-58C helicopters with flat-pane canopies to reduce glint and make the machines harder to see by eye or by radar, infra-red suppression, protective features against ground fire and extra equipment, the usual armament being a 7.62-mm (0.3-in) machine-gun. In 1981 Bell won the AHIP (Army Helicopter Improvement Programme), which from 1983 is expected to lead to a $2 billion job rebuilding 578 Kiowas to OH-58D standard with a 650-hp (485-kW) Allison engine, new four-blade rotor and a mass of new equipment including an MMS (Mast-Mounted Sight).

Since the late 1950s every helicopter pilot has known that for battlefield use it is essential to have a sight system which can give a view of the enemy that can be magnified, that will function by night

USA no. 16695 was built as a Bell OH-58A Kiowa and funded in the 1968 fiscal year, later being given the M27 kit which adds a 7.62-mm (0.3-in) M134 Minigun on the left side with 2,000 rounds. An initial 275 of these agile machines are being rebuilt by Bell's Amarillo facility to OH-58C standard with an uprated engine, flat-plate canopy and improved equipment.

Egypt was one of the overseas customers for the extremely large Mil Mi-6 heavy cargo and assault helicopter, which in many countries also plays an important role in opening up undeveloped regions. Typical loads include 90 troops or 41 stretcher casualties.

Approximately 50 Soviet-supplied Mil Mi-8T assault helicopters remain operational with the Egyptian air force, providing a substantial force of tough machines with experienced crews. At least 20 were lost in accidents and warfare, but their exploits in depositing missile teams behind the Bar-Lev line, and in direct armed assault, have become textbook material for all tactical helicopter operators.

Approximately 50 Soviet-supplied Mil Mi-8T assault helicopters remain operational with the Egyptian air force, providing a substantial force of tough machines with experienced crews. At least 20 were lost in accidents and warfare, but their exploits in depositing missile teams behind the Bar-Lev line, and in direct armed assault, have become textbook material for all tactical helicopter operators.

Larger and more powerful than the Westland Sea King, the Mil Mi-8 has been built in far greater numbers than any other helicopter of its size, total deliveries by 1983 exceeding 8,100. Finland's air force received both the Mi-8, shown here, and the much more common Mi-8T utility model with round windows. The weather radar pod was installed after delivery.

or in bad weather and which will if possible see through dust or smoke. These demands alone are difficult enough, but it is also self-evident that, just as a periscope enables an observer to hide in a trench, so a high-mounted sight enables a helicopter to keep low down out of sight behind trees, buildings or other cover. Amazingly, extremely costly helicopters are still being built with the sight as low as possible in the tip of the nose, so that (as the machine cannot fly inverted) the entire helicopter must expose itself to the enemy for the sight to be used. Fortunately since 1979 a growing number of army machines have been fitted with an MMS, typically incorporating magnifying optics, TV and FLIR (forward-looking infra-red). Pilots also increasingly wear night-vision goggles, and in the cleverest machines a helmet-mounted sight system cues the weapons automatically to wherever the wearer is looking.

Flying cranes

Warsaw Pact forces took a long time to produce sophisticated helicopters, but from the early 1950s their machines were powerful and capable even in the harshest conditions. The giant Mil Mi-6 served alongside the 1,700-hp (1268-kW) Mi-4 and 3,400-hp (2535-kW) Yak-24, and from the early 1960s the most common machine has been the Mi-8 (called 'Hip' by NATO). The first Mi-8 had a single 2,700-hp (2013-kW) engine, but production machines have two 1,700-hp (1268-kW) turbines and a cabin big enough for 28 troops. Moreover, several tactical versions have devastating external armament, a typical kit being a heavy machine-gun (12.7 mm/0.5 in) in the nose, 192 rockets in six launch pods plus four 'AT-2' or 'AT-3' guided anti-tank rockets! The Mi-17 has uprated 2,200-hp (1640-kW) engines and better performance. By 1983 production of the Mi-8 alone had almost reached 8,000, of which some 7,000 are military.

Aérospatiale SA 321L Super Frelon of the Libyan air force, which has bought nine of the type.

Sikorsky H-53 Stallion

History and Notes

With the company designation S-65, this family of transport helicopters began as a very capable machine designed as an assault transport for the US Marine Corps, with two 2,850-hp (2126-kW) engines, and today has grown into the most powerful helicopter outside the Soviet Union with three 4,380-hp (3267-kW) engines! A natural scale-up of the S-61, but without a boat hull, the original CH-53A flew on 14 October 1964, and eventually 139 of this model were supplied. The standard CH-53A carries an 8,000-lb (3628-kg) cargo load or 38 troops or 24 stretcher (litter) casualties and four attendants, but 15 were transferred to the US Navy as MCM (mine countermeasures) sweeping machines and five to the USAF. For Vietnam, the HH-53B Super Jolly (Green) was fitted with extra

fuel, armour, defensive guns and other weapons, rescue hoist and inflight refuelling probe, the CH-53C being the plain transport counterpart. The CH-53D has 3,925-hp (2928-kW) engines, and 126 were built for the US Marines with 55 troop seats; 153 were assembled in Germany for army use and Austria bought the CH-53Ö. The HH-53H is the USAF 'Pave Low 3' night/all-weather rescue model with extremely comprehensive navaids and avionics. By far the most powerful, the US Marines' CH-53E Super Stallion has three engines driving a main rotor with seven titanium/glassfibre blades and many other changes. Since 1981 this model has been delivered also to the US Navy, for ship delivery and clearing carrier decks or enemy territory of crashed aircraft.

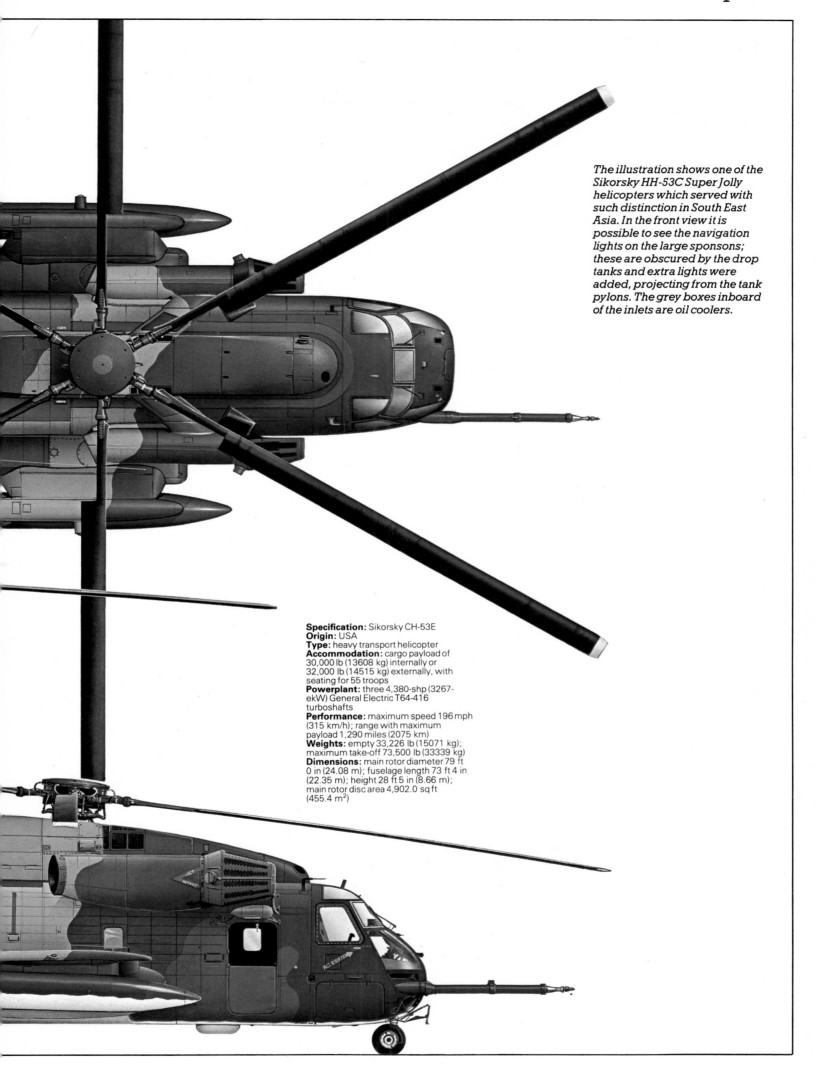

The illustration shows one of the Sikorsky HH-53C Super Jolly helicopters which served with such distinction in South East Asia. In the front view it is possible to see the navigation lights on the large sponsons; these are obscured by the drop tanks and extra lights were added, projecting from the tank pylons. The grey boxes inboard of the inlets are oil coolers.

Specification: Sikorsky CH-53E
Origin: USA
Type: heavy transport helicopter
Accommodation: cargo payload of 30,000 lb (13608 kg) internally or 32,000 lb (14515 kg) externally, with seating for 55 troops
Powerplant: three 4,380-shp (3267-ekW) General Electric T64-416 turboshafts
Performance: maximum speed 196 mph (315 km/h); range with maximum payload 1,290 miles (2075 km)
Weights: empty 33,226 lb (15071 kg); maximum take-off 73,500 lb (33339 kg)
Dimensions: main rotor diameter 79 ft 0 in (24.08 m); fuselage length 73 ft 4 in (22.35 m); height 28 ft 5 in (8.66 m); main rotor disc area 4,902.0 sq ft (455.4 m²)

Sikorsky CH-53D assigned to HMH-462 Marine Heavy Helicopter Squadron based at Futenma, Okinawa, painted in

the usual overall green but with the recently standardized low-visibility national insignia.

Sikorsky CH-53E Super Stallion

1 Retractable inflight refuelling boom
2 Refuelling boom fairing
3 Instrument compartment access door
4 Glideslope aerial
5 Fresh air intakes
6 Yaw control rudder pedals
7 Landing lamp
8 Downward vision windows
9 Nose undercarriage leg strut
10 Twin nosewheels
11 Radio and electronics bays, port and starboard
12 Cockpit floor level
13 Collective pitch control lever
14 Cyclic pitch control column
15 Co-pilot's armoured seat
16 Instrument panel shroud
17 Windscreen wipers
18 Windscreen panels
19 Rescue hoist/winch
20 Pitot tube
21 UHF aerial
22 Overhead control panel
23 Pilot's armoured seat
24 Cockpit eyebrow window
25 Flight leader's folding jump seat
26 Cockpit bulkhead
27 Jettisonable side window panel
28 Starboard side crew entry door
29 Fuselage and stringer construction
30 Emergency exit window
31 Engine air intake particle separator
32 Bevel drive gearbox
33 Engine oil cooler
34 Auxiliary power unit (APU)
35 Cabin heater unit
36 Starboard engine intake particle separator
37 Engine cowlings, armoured on lower surface
38 Auxiliary gearbox
39 Hydraulic reservoirs
40 Gearbox drive shaft
41 Port engine transmission shaft
42 Folding troop seats, maximum 37 troops
43 Cargo loading floor
44 Roller conveyor
45 Cargo hook support links
46 General Electric T64-GE-415 turboshaft engine
47 Gearbox mounting fuselage main frame
48 Engine exhaust duct
49 Centre engine intake
50 Main transmission gearbox
51 Blade pitch control rotating swashplate
52 Rotor head mechanism
53 Blade pitch control links
54 Blade folding hinge points
55 Rotor head fairing
56 Seven-blade main rotor, 79-ft (24.08-m) diameter
57 Centre engine oil cooler
58 Maintenance handrail

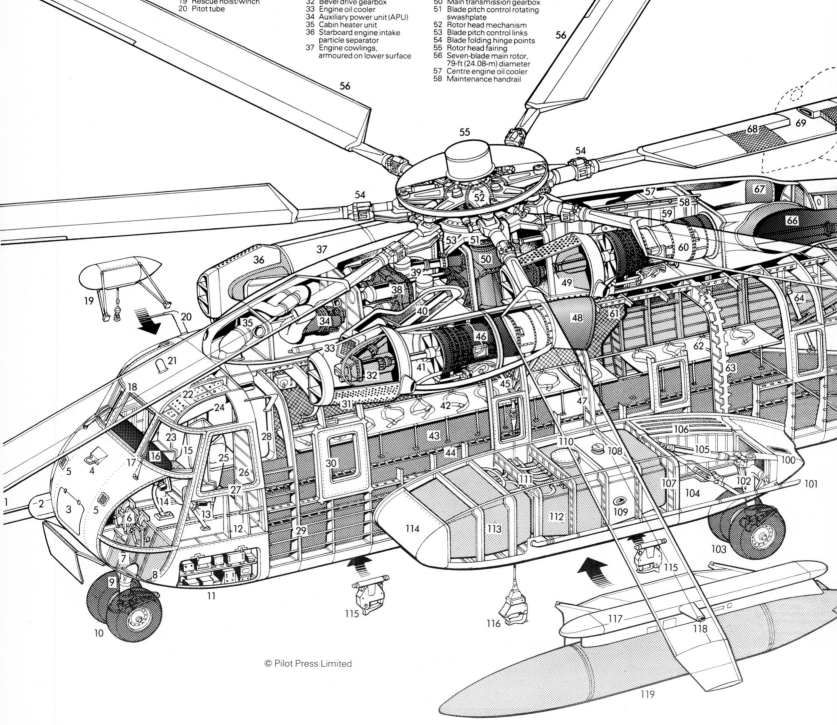

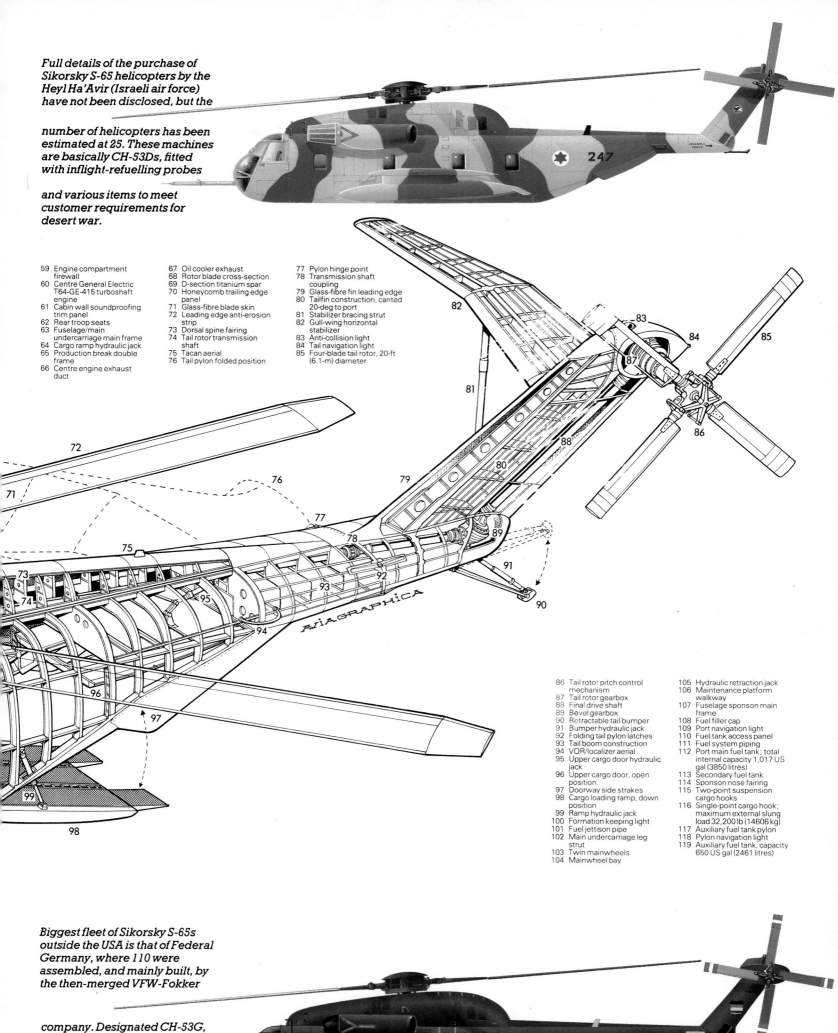

Full details of the purchase of Sikorsky S-65 helicopters by the Heyl Ha'Avir (Israeli air force) have not been disclosed, but the

number of helicopters has been estimated at 25. These machines are basically CH-53Ds, fitted with inflight-refuelling probes

and various items to meet customer requirements for desert war.

59 Engine compartment firewall
60 Centre General Electric T64-GE-415 turboshaft engine
61 Cabin wall soundproofing trim panel
62 Rear troop seats
63 Fuselage/main undercarriage main frame
64 Cargo ramp hydraulic jack
65 Production break double frame
66 Centre engine exhaust duct

67 Oil cooler exhaust
68 Rotor blade cross-section
69 D-section titanium spar
70 Honeycomb trailing edge panel
71 Glass-fibre blade skin
72 Leading edge anti-erosion strip
73 Dorsal spine fairing
74 Tail rotor transmission shaft
75 Tacan aerial
76 Tail pylon folded position

77 Pylon hinge point
78 Transmission shaft coupling
79 Glass-fibre fin leading edge
80 Tailfin construction, canted 20-deg to port
81 Stabilizer bracing strut
82 Gull-wing horizontal stabilizer
83 Anti-collision light
84 Tail navigation light
85 Four-blade tail rotor, 20-ft (6.1-m) diameter

86 Tail rotor pitch control mechanism
87 Tail rotor gearbox
88 Final drive shaft
89 Bevel gearbox
90 Retractable tail bumper
91 Bumper hydraulic jack
92 Folding tail pylon latches
93 Tail boom construction
94 VOR/localizer aerial
95 Upper cargo door hydraulic jack
96 Upper cargo door, open position
97 Doorway side strakes
98 Cargo loading ramp, down position
99 Ramp hydraulic jack
100 Formation keeping light
101 Fuel jettison pipe
102 Main undercarriage leg strut
103 Twin mainwheels
104 Mainwheel bay

105 Hydraulic retraction jack
106 Maintenance platform walkway
107 Fuselage sponson main frame
108 Fuel filler cap
109 Port navigation light
110 Fuel tank access panel
111 Fuel system piping
112 Port main fuel tank; total internal capacity 1,017 US gal (3850 litres)
113 Secondary fuel tank
114 Sponson nose fairing
115 Two-point suspension cargo hooks
116 Single-point cargo hook; maximum external slung load 32,200 lb (14606 kg)
117 Auxiliary fuel tank pylon
118 Pylon navigation light
119 Auxiliary fuel tank, capacity 650 US gal (2461 litres)

Biggest fleet of Sikorsky S-65s outside the USA is that of Federal Germany, where 110 were assembled, and mainly built, by the then-merged VFW-Fokker

company. Designated CH-53G, they were assigned to the army, as is this example, and to the Luftwaffe. FR probes and engine inlet particle-separators are not fitted.

Helicopters of the World

Since delivery all Sikorsky CH-54 Tarhe crane helicopters of the US Army have been fitted with large inlet filters to screen out sand, dust and other foreign material from the T73 engines. This is a CH-54A with single main wheels.

The Mil design bureau also produced a powerful crane helicopter, the Mi-10K and Mi-10 series, designed for lifting and positioning very heavy loads and using rotors and engines similar to those of the Mi-6, but these are seldom used by military units. In contrast, the US Army followed the large Sikorsky H-37 (later CH-37) Mojave, which carried 26 troops, 24 stretcher (litter) casualties or three Jeeps, with the much more capable Sikorsky S-64, which it designated CH-54 Tarhe. The Tarhe is the only crane helicopter in service in the West, and the 100-odd built are in frequent demand for hire for civilian purposes. Powered by two 4,500-hp (3356-kW) or 4,800-hp (3579-kW) Pratt & Whitney turbines, the Tarhe has no fuselage but just a strong beam carrying the cockpit under the front and the tailfin and rotor at the back. Under it can be slung various loads weighing up to 22,000 lb (9979 kg) (40,780 lb/18497 kg) has been lifted, but that was exceptional). In Vietnam, Tarhes were credited with bringing back 380 shot-down aircraft, saving a claimed $210 million. Special vans can be clipped on housing freight, troops (up to 87 in an emergency) or even an equipped surgical hospital.

Sikorsky's next machine, the S-65, was described in the preceding chapter; it is used not only by the US Navy and Marines, the latter for assault in amphibious warfare, but also by the Federal German Army for whom 153 were assembled in Germany. In this top category of size and power the chief army airlift helicopter outside the Soviet Union is the Boeing Vertol CH-47 Chinook. First flown in September 1961, the Chinook follows the usual Vertol tandem-rotor configuration, with the two three-bladed intermeshing rotors driven by two 2,200-hp (1640-kW) Lycoming T55 engines on the sides of the large rear fin. The body has an ideal box-like form, with interior width 7 ft 6 in (2.28 m) and height 6 ft 6 in (2 m) and a full-width rear ramp door for loading small vehicles or for paradropping various loads. External cargo up to a weight of 28,000 lb (12700kg) can be carried, and seating can be installed for 44 troops (though in an emergency a Chinook rescued 147 civilians). In the casevac role 24 litters (stretchers) and attendants can be accommodated, and

There are few US Army loads that cannot be lifted by the CH-54 Tarhe, except for armour. This is a CH-54A, most of which have today been fitted with large inlet filters ahead of the two 4,500-hp engines. The planned replacement, the CH-62, has been on ice for eight years, though since 1980 a little funding has been trickling through to develop the transmission.

Delivery of a slung load by a Sikorsky CH-54A Tarhe of the US Army. This 9,000-hp (6714-kW) crane helicopter has proved extremely useful, to the extent that the USA units have been inundated with requests for hire by civilian groups needing a heavy load moved short distances.

there are many special-role fittings available. Over its 20-year life the Chinook has been kept the same size but progressively uprated in power (to 4,500 hp (3356 kW) per engine) and capability, and almost 1,000 have been produced, including well over 200 licence-built by Meridionali in Italy. Britain sent four of its 36 almost new and extremely well equipped Chinooks to the South Atlantic in April 1982, but three were lost aboard the *Atlantic Conveyor*; the sole survivor performed prodigious feats flying literally round the clock, often in range of hostile fire.

From the earliest days of helicopters used in support of land battles it had been evident that they could carry small missiles in the anti-armour role and a diverse range of weapons in the assault,

Boeing Vertol CH-47 Chinook

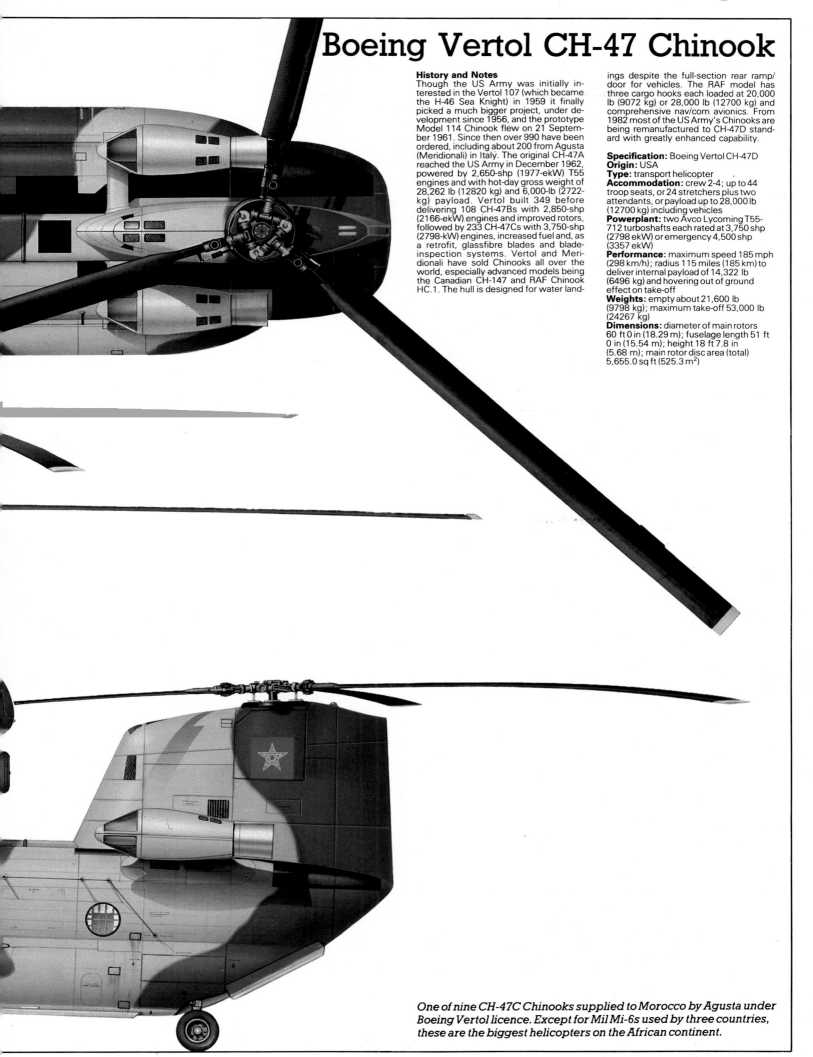

History and Notes
Though the US Army was initially interested in the Vertol 107 (which became the H-46 Sea Knight) in 1959 it finally picked a much bigger project, under development since 1956, and the prototype Model 114 Chinook flew on 21 September 1961. Since then over 990 have been ordered, including about 200 from Agusta (Meridionali) in Italy. The original CH-47A reached the US Army in December 1962, powered by 2,650-shp (1977-ekW) T55 engines and with hot-day gross weight of 28,262 lb (12820 kg) and 6,000-lb (2722-kg) payload. Vertol built 349 before delivering 108 CH-47Bs with 2,850-shp (2166-ekW) engines and improved rotors, followed by 233 CH-47Cs with 3,750-shp (2798-kW) engines, increased fuel and, as a retrofit, glassfibre blades and blade-inspection systems. Vertol and Meridionali have sold Chinooks all over the world, especially advanced models being the Canadian CH-147 and RAF Chinook HC.1. The hull is designed for water landings despite the full-section rear ramp/door for vehicles. The RAF model has three cargo hooks each loaded at 20,000 lb (9072 kg) or 28,000 lb (12700 kg) and comprehensive nav/com avionics. From 1982 most of the US Army's Chinooks are being remanufactured to CH-47D standard with greatly enhanced capability.

Specification: Boeing Vertol CH-47D
Origin: USA
Type: transport helicopter
Accommodation: crew 2-4; up to 44 troop seats, or 24 stretchers plus two attendants, or payload up to 28,000 lb (12700 kg) including vehicles
Powerplant: two Avco Lycoming T55-712 turboshafts each rated at 3,750 shp (2798 ekW) or emergency 4,500 shp (3357 ekW)
Performance: maximum speed 185 mph (298 km/h); radius 115 miles (185 km) to deliver internal payload of 14,322 lb (6496 kg) and hovering out of ground effect on take-off
Weights: empty about 21,600 lb (9798 kg); maximum take-off 53,000 lb (24267 kg)
Dimensions: diameter of main rotors 60 ft 0 in (18.29 m); fuselage length 51 ft 0 in (15.54 m); height 18 ft 7.8 in (5.68 m); main rotor disc area (total) 5,655.0 sq ft (525.3 m²)

One of nine CH-47C Chinooks supplied to Morocco by Agusta under Boeing Vertol licence. Except for Mil Mi-6s used by three countries, these are the biggest helicopters on the African continent.

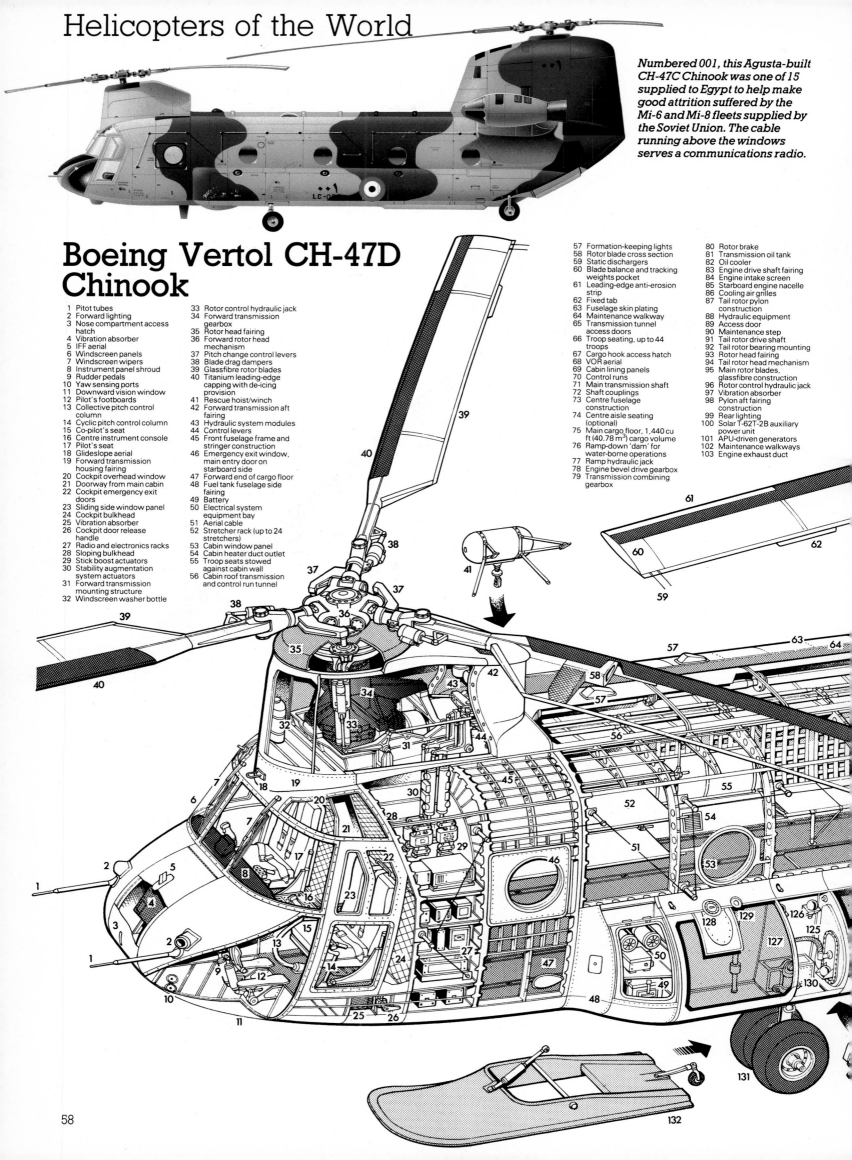

Numbered 001, this Agusta-built CH-47C Chinook was one of 15 supplied to Egypt to help make good attrition suffered by the Mi-6 and Mi-8 fleets supplied by the Soviet Union. The cable running above the windows serves a communications radio.

Boeing Vertol CH-47D Chinook

1 Pitot tubes
2 Forward lighting
3 Nose compartment access hatch
4 Vibration absorber
5 IFF aerial
6 Windscreen panels
7 Windscreen wipers
8 Instrument panel shroud
9 Rudder pedals
10 Yaw sensing ports
11 Downward vision window
12 Pilot's footboards
13 Collective pitch control column
14 Cyclic pitch control column
15 Co-pilot's seat
16 Centre instrument console
17 Pilot's seat
18 Glideslope aerial
19 Forward transmission housing fairing
20 Cockpit overhead window
21 Doorway from main cabin
22 Cockpit emergency exit doors
23 Sliding side window panel
24 Cockpit bulkhead
25 Vibration absorber
26 Cockpit door release handle
27 Radio and electronics racks
28 Sloping bulkhead
29 Stick boost actuators
30 Stability augmentation system actuators
31 Forward transmission mounting structure
32 Windscreen washer bottle

33 Rotor control hydraulic jack
34 Forward transmission gearbox
35 Rotor head fairing
36 Forward rotor head mechanism
37 Pitch change control levers
38 Blade drag dampers
39 Glassfibre rotor blades
40 Titanium leading-edge capping with de-icing provision
41 Rescue hoist/winch
42 Forward transmission aft fairing
43 Hydraulic system modules
44 Control levers
45 Front fuselage frame and stringer construction
46 Emergency exit window, main entry door on starboard side
47 Forward end of cargo floor
48 Fuel tank fuselage side fairing
49 Battery
50 Electrical system equipment bay
51 Aerial cable
52 Stretcher rack (up to 24 stretchers)
53 Cabin window panel
54 Cabin heater duct outlet
55 Troop seats stowed against cabin wall
56 Cabin roof transmission and control run tunnel

57 Formation-keeping lights
58 Rotor blade cross section
59 Static dischargers
60 Blade balance and tracking weights pocket
61 Leading-edge anti-erosion strip
62 Fixed tab
63 Fuselage skin plating
64 Maintenance walkway
65 Transmission tunnel access doors
66 Troop seating, up to 44 troops
67 Cargo hook access hatch
68 VOR aerial
69 Cabin lining panels
70 Control runs
71 Main transmission shaft
72 Shaft couplings
73 Centre fuselage construction
74 Centre aisle seating (optional)
75 Main cargo floor, 1,440 cu ft (40.78 m³) cargo volume
76 Ramp-down 'dam' for water-borne operations
77 Ramp hydraulic jack
78 Engine bevel drive gearbox
79 Transmission combining gearbox

80 Rotor brake
81 Transmission oil tank
82 Oil cooler
83 Engine drive shaft fairing
84 Engine intake screen
85 Starboard engine nacelle
86 Cooling air grilles
87 Tail rotor pylon construction
88 Hydraulic equipment
89 Access door
90 Maintenance step
91 Tail rotor drive shaft
92 Tail rotor bearing mounting
93 Rotor head fairing
94 Tail rotor head mechanism
95 Main rotor blades, glassfibre construction
96 Rotor control hydraulic jack
97 Vibration absorber
98 Pylon aft fairing construction
99 Rear lighting
100 Solar T-62T-2B auxiliary power unit
101 APU-driven generators
102 Maintenance walkways
103 Engine exhaust duct

Battlefield Helicopters

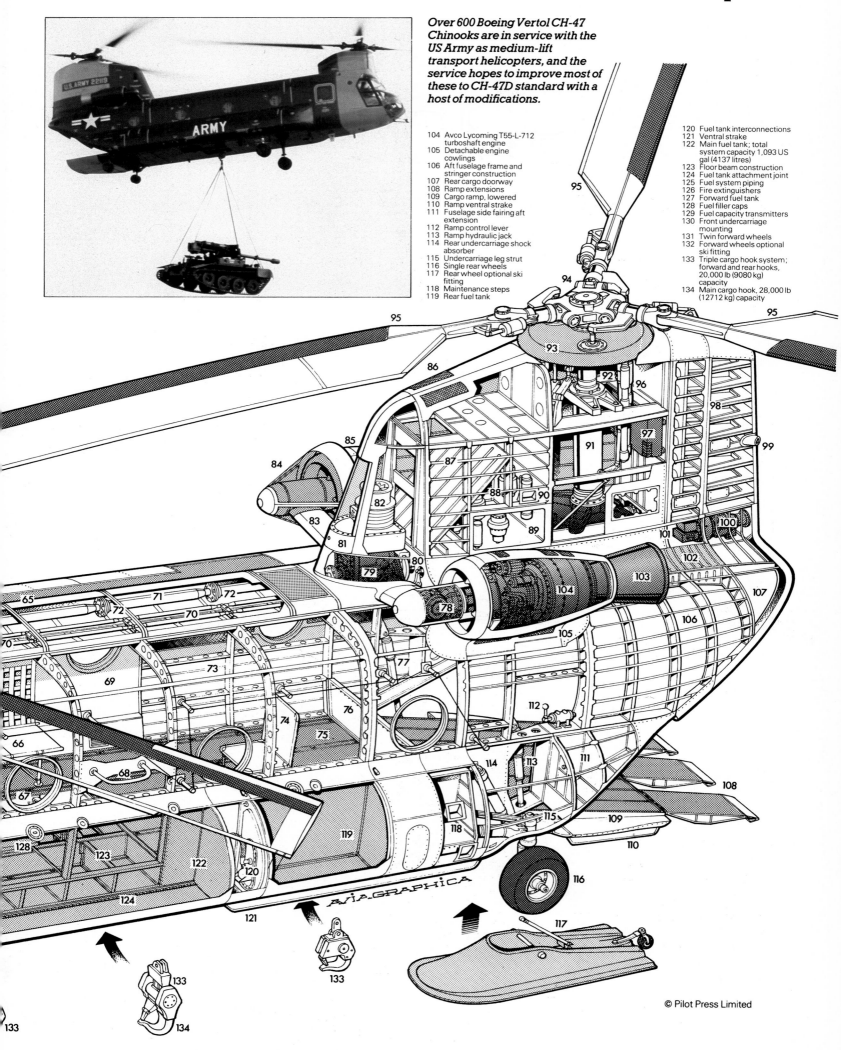

Over 600 Boeing Vertol CH-47 Chinooks are in service with the US Army as medium-lift transport helicopters, and the service hopes to improve most of these to CH-47D standard with a host of modifications.

104 Avco Lycoming T55-L-712 turboshaft engine
105 Detachable engine cowlings
106 Aft fuselage frame and stringer construction
107 Rear cargo doorway
108 Ramp extensions
109 Cargo ramp, lowered
110 Ramp ventral strake
111 Fuselage side fairing aft extension
112 Ramp control lever
113 Ramp hydraulic jack
114 Rear undercarriage shock absorber
115 Undercarriage leg strut
116 Single rear wheels
117 Rear wheel optional ski fitting
118 Maintenance steps
119 Rear fuel tank

120 Fuel tank interconnections
121 Ventral strake
122 Main fuel tank; total system capacity 1,093 US gal (4137 litres)
123 Floor beam construction
124 Fuel tank attachment joint
125 Fuel system piping
126 Fire extinguishers
127 Forward fuel tank
128 Fuel filler caps
129 Fuel capacity transmitters
130 Front undercarriage mounting
131 Twin forward wheels
132 Forward wheels optional ski fitting
133 Triple cargo hook system; forward and rear hooks, 20,000 lb (9080 kg) capacity
134 Main cargo hook, 28,000 lb (12712 kg) capacity

AVIA.GRAPHICA

© Pilot Press Limited

59

Helicopters of the World

The Bell AH-1 HueyCobras of the US Marine Corps can be visually identified by the much taller rear engine section housing the T400 twin coupled-turbine powerplant. This AH-1J SeaCobra has had the N197 three-barrel 20-mm cannon removed from its chin turret and is seen operating from a ship during an amphibious assault. The later AH-1T has higher performance and more advanced weapons.

escort and fire support roles. Early anti-armour helicopters were merely small existing machines, such as the Aérospatiale Alouette, fitted with a sight system and two or four wire-guided missiles. It was soon clear that the key item for development was the sight, which has to be stabilized against sudden tilting or vibration, and give a clear magnified picture of the target under the worst conditions. As noted previously the sight gradually migrated from being low on the nose to the cabin roof and finally to a mast above the rotor, where it can survey the enemy without exposing the helicopter. Such dedicated machines usually carry just the missiles visible externally, ready to fire, but a few carry reloads in the cabin and an alternative scheme is to use the helicopter as a transport for anti-tank infantry teams which can be landed at tactical spots, moved to and fro and kept supplied with fresh missiles.

There are more than 20 types of helicopter used in the anti-tank role, and more than 20

Air Vehicle 06, the sixth pre-production Hughes YAH-64 Apache, seen on test at minimum 'nap of the Earth' height in 1982. Totally different in almost every detail from the original Hughes prototypes which won the development contract for this important machine from the USA, the definitive version is unfortunately much more costly, unit price in production being substantially higher than $10 million. Total procurement may reach 446.

Hughes AH-64 Apache

History and Notes
Designed in 1972-3 to meet the US Army's need for an AAH (Advanced Attack Helicopter), the AH-64A beat a Bell competitor which had reversed the traditional Cobra arrangement of seating the pilot above and behind the co-pilot/gunner, an arrangement maintained by Hughes. Features include two T700 engines flat-rated to provide high emergency power and with large IR-suppressing exhaust systems, a large flat-plate canopy with boron armour, multi-spar stainless steel and glassfibre rotor blades designed to withstand 23-mm hits, extremely comprehensive avionics and weapon fits, and numerous crash-resistant features to protect the crew. Development was unfortunately prolonged, so that inflation has multiplied the price and not all the planned 536 Apaches may be funded. Appearance changed dramatically during development, especially at the nose and tail, and the nose carries Martin Marietta TADS/PNVS (Target Acquisition and Designation Sight/Pilot's Night Vision System). New missiles became available, and as well as laser designation and ranging an IHADSS (Integrated Helmet And Display Sighting System) is fitted, both crew members being able to acquire targets by head movement. The first YAH-64 flew on 30 September 1975 and production delivery was due in December 1983.

Specification: Hughes AH-64
Origin: USA
Type: armed battlefield helicopter
Accommodation: two
Armament: one 30-mm Hughes Chain Gun with 1,200 rounds and remote aiming; four stub-wing hardpoints for normal anti-armour load of 16 Hellfire missiles (initially with laser guidance);

other loads can include four 18-round pods of 2.75-in (69.9-mm) rockets
Powerplant: two 1,536-shp (1146-ekW) General Electric T700-700 turboshafts
Performance: maximum speed (at 13,925 lb/6316 kg) 192mph (309 km/h); range (internal fuel) 380 miles (611 km), and (ferry) 1,121 miles (1804 km)
Weights: empty 10,268 lb (4657 kg); maximum take-off 17,650 lb (8006 kg)
Dimensions: main rotor diameter 48 ft 0 in (14.63 m); fuselage length 49 ft 1½ in (14.97 m); height 13 ft 10 in (4.22 m); main rotor disc area 1,809.5 sq ft (168.11 m²)

The Hughes AH-64 Apache, certainly the most expensive vehicle ever proposed for use in a land battle.

Hughes AH-64 Apache

A prototype YAH-64 Apache tests its rocket launchers.

Hughes anti-tank TOW Defender in action. The TOW missile is just emerging from the no. 3 launch tube.

air-launched anti-tank missile types. All the early models used optical tracking of the target and direct operator command guidance with signals transmitted along fine current-carrying wires. More recent weapons home automatically by laser, millimetre-wave radar or infra-red, dispensing with wires and enabling missile speed to be greatly increased, and in most cases the range also to

Hughes 500 Defender

History and Notes
In 1965 the US Army held an LOH (Light Observation Helicopter) contest, with potential production for a four-figure total. When the Hughes OH-6A Cayuse won there was a storm, it being claimed the company was selling below cost. Despite this, 1,415 OH-6s gave splendid service in Vietnam, and as its tadpole shape was extremely compact, and performance on a 317 shp (236-ekW) Allison engine the highest in its class, it was popular. From it Hughes developed a family of Model 500s, the basic Model 500 with improved 317-shp (236-ekW) engine being sold to nine countries and licence-made in Argentina and Japan. The Model 500MD has the more powerful C20B engine and can have self-sealing tanks, inlet particle filter, IR-suppressing exhausts, and many role fits including seven seats, or two stretchers and two attendants, or various weapons. Licensed production proceeds at BredaNardi (Italy) and KAL (South Korea). The Model 500MD Scout Defender is the basic armed version, and a sub-type has the MMS (mast-mounted sight) for 'hull down' surveillance or missile guidance, and quiet-running features. TOW Defenders have four TOW missiles, original deliveries having a nose sight. ASW Defenders have search radar, towed MAD, hauldown ship gear, pop-out flotation bags and other naval equipment. The Defender II is an updated multi-role model now being delivered with quiet rotors, MMS, IR suppression, FLIR (forward-looking IR) night vision and many other devices including APR-39 passive radar warning.

Specification: Hughes Model 500MD Defender II
Origin: USA
Type: multi-role combat helicopter
Accommodation: two
Armament: options include Hughes 30-mm Chain Gun (firing rate reduced to 350

A worldwide best-seller, the Hughes Model 500 Defender family are all amazingly agile and compact, with a main-rotor diameter of only 26 ft (8 m). This is one of 15 500MD TOW Defenders for Kenya, with TOW sight on the nose.

rounds per minute), four TOW missiles and two Stinger MLMS AAMs
Powerplant: one 420-shp (313-ekW) Allison 250-C20B turboshaft
Performance: maximum speed 152 mph (217 km/h); range 366 miles (589 km)
Weights: empty typically 1,260 lb (572 kg); maximum take-off 3,000 lb (1361 kg)
Dimensions: main rotor diameter 26 ft 4¾ in (8.05 m); fuselage length 23 ft 0 in (7.01 m); height 8 ft 10¾ in (2.71 m); main rotor disc area 545.0 sq ft (50.7 m²)

Hughes 500MD Defender

Hughes 500MD Defender launching a TOW missile.

be extended (typically to 2½ miles/4 km). Such systems are still compact and light enough to be added to almost any army helicopter, usually with four to eight ready-fire rounds.

The armed helicopter itself, however, underwent a major metamorphosis in the early 1960s when it was realized that, instead of just adding weapons to a transport or utility helicopter, the helicopter itself could be designed purely as a fighting machine. The first such 'gunship' was the US Army Lockheed AH-56A Cheyenne AAFSS (Advanced Aerial Fire-Support System) which was picked over its rivals in March 1966. Powered by a 3,925-hp (2927-kW) T64 engine, driving not only a rigid main rotor and anti-torque tail rotor but also a pusher propeller to increase speed to 244 mph (393 km/h), the Cheyenne had a slim body with a fighter-type cockpit for a gunner in the nose and a pilot above and to the rear. The helicopter bristled with complex avionics and weapons, but eventually proved just too difficult and too expensive. In its place came the privately developed Bell AH-1 HueyCobra, which simply put a slim gunship body on the existing Huey rotor system, and less complex sensors and weapons.

Thousands of Cobras were built, large numbers even getting into the Vietnam war where they served with conspicuous success alongside the small Hughes OH-6A Cayuse observation machine, itself armed and armoured and popularly called the Loach, from LOH (Light Observation Helicopter). Today the Cobra is still in production, and large numbers of earlier models are being rebuilt with better avionics and weapons and many new features including a flat-plate canopy to improve resistance to bullets and reduce 'glint' and battlefield visibility. As a harder-hitting

Right: Though relatively expensive, the MBB BO 105 has the advantages of twin engines, exceptional agility and an extremely high standard of avionics and other equipment. One of the few armed versions is the BO 105P, selected as PAH-1 (anti-tank helicopter type 1) by the West German army. Six HOT missiles are carried in their sealed tubes on outrigger pylons, the stabilized sight being mounted in the cabin roof. Other special equipment in this version includes the Singer ASN-128 Doppler navigator. The 212 on order were all delivered by mid-1983.

Supplementing an even larger force of Alouettes, the Royal Netherlands army No. 300 Squadron at Deelen has 30 of these BO 105C multi-role machines. Flight crews are provided by the KLu (air force).

Bell Model 209 HueyCobra

History and Notes
Bell developed the Model 209 as an urgent company-funded programme to provide a cheaper alternative to the problem-ridden AH-56A, and once the prototype had flown on 7 September 1965 its future was assured. Based on the Model 204, the Model 209 had a new slim fuselage with a fighter-type cockpit for the pilot high in the rear and a co-pilot/gunner lower in the front directing the fire of a wide range of weapons mounted on lateral stub wings or under the nose. The AH-1G HueyCobra went into production in 1966 and over 1,000 were delivered in the first four years.

Powered by a 1,400-shp (1044-ekW) T53, the AH-1G saw extensive service in Vietnam. Many were converted as TH-1G dual trainers. The Spanish navy Z.14 version is used for anti-ship attack. The AH-1J SeaCobra was the first twin-engine version, for the US Marine Corps, with an 1,800-shp (1343-ekW) T400 installation;

Spurred by the insatiable demands of the Vietnam War, Bell AH-1G HueyCobra helicopters were bought in quantities almost as large as the basic UH-1D and UH-1H from fiscal year 1966 onwards (the year does not appear in the serial number). This early example has the standard M28 chin turret with an M134 Minigun with 4,000 rounds of 7.62-mm (0.3-in) ammunition and an M129 grenade-launcher with 300 grenades of 40-mm (1.58-in) calibre. It is also shown with pairs of M157 (seven 2.75-in/70-mm) and M159C (19 2.75-in/70-mm) rocket-launchers.

in 1974-5 a batch of 202 with TOW missiles was supplied to Iran. The AH-1Q was an interim US Army version with TOW missiles, while the AH-1R has the 1,800-shp (1343-ekW) T53-703 engine. The current USA model is the AH-1S, produced in three successively improved stages ending with flat-plate canopies. TOW missiles and over 80 new or improved items of avionics and equipment for all-weather flying at almost ground level. The current USMC model is the AH-1T Improved SeaCobra with longer fuselage, TOW missiles and 1,970-shp (1470-ekW) T400 engine group. One AH-1T has twin T700-700 engines of 3,200 shp (2387 ekW) and it is proposed to retrofit the USMC force with the T700-401, giving no less than 3,380 shp (2521 ekW).

Specification: Bell AH-1S
Origin: USA
Type: anti-armour attack helicopter
Accommodation: pilot and co-pilot/gunner
Armament: eight TOW missiles on outboard wing points, with pods inboard housing groups of 7 or 19 of any of five types of 2.75-in (69.9-mm) rocket; General Electric turret under nose with M197 20-mm three-barrel gun (alternatives are 30-mm gun or combined 7.62-mm (0.3-in) Minigun plus 40-mm grenade-launcher)
Powerplant: one 1,800-shp (1343-ekW) Avco Lycoming T53-703 turboshaft
Performance: maximum speed varies from 207 mph (333 km/h) to 141 mph (227 km/h) depending on equipment fit; range at sea level with maximum fuel and 8 per cent reserves 315 miles (507 km)
Weights: empty 6,479 lb (2939 kg); maximum take-off 10,000 lb (4535 kg)
Dimensions: main rotor diameter 44 ft 0 in (13.41 m) or, in AH-1T family, 48 ft 0 in (14.63 m); fuselage length 44 ft 7 in (13.59 m) or, in AH-1T, 48 ft 2 in (14.68 m); height over tail rotor 13 ft 6¼ in (4.12 m); main rotor disc area 1,520.5 sq ft (141.26 m²) or, in AH-1T, 1,809.6 sq ft (168.1 m²)

UNITED STATES ARMY

DANGER

16369

Aérospatiale/Westland Gazelle

History and Notes

Though distantly derived from the Alouette, the Gazelle differs in having a completely streamlined stressed-skin fuselage and cabin for side-by-side pilots with dual controls. The first production SA 341 flew on 6 August 1971, and featured the Bölkow-developed rigid main rotor and Aérospatiale *fenestron* shrouded tail rotor in a duct built into the fin. As part of the 1967 agreement with the UK many early Gazelles were assembled and partly built by Westland for the British Army (AH.Mk 1), RN (HT.Mk 2) and RAF (HT.Mk 3). The Gazelle AH.1 has Doppler, auto-chart display and (optionally) TOW missiles and roof sight; the HT variants have a stab-augmentation system, the naval Gazelle HT.Mk 2 also having a rescue hoist. The SA 341F is the basic ALAT (French Army light aviation) model. The SA 341H military export version is licence-built by Soko of Yugoslavia. The SA 342 introduced an Astazou engine uprated from 590 to 859 shp (440 to 641 ekW) and an improved *fenestron* permitting weight to be increased. Of several military SA 342 versions, ALAT is buying 120 of the SA 342M model with advanced avionics and four HOT missile tubes with a stabilized sight on the roof. Total sales of all versions reached 1,000 by 1983,

Specification: Aérospatiale SA 342L
Origin: France
Type: military utility helicopter
Accommodation: two pilots in front with optional bench seat behind for three which folds down for cargo carrying; sling for 1,543 lb (700 kg) and hoist for 300 lb (135 kg)
Accommodation: two pilots in front, guns or 20-mm cannon, two pods of 2.75-in or 68-mm rockets, four/six HOT

missiles, or four AS.11 or two AS.12 missiles
Powerplant: one 859-shp (641-ekW) Turboméca Astazou XIV turboshaft
Performance: maximum speed 193 mph (310 km/h); cruising speed 148 mph (238 km/h); range with 1,102-lb (500-kg) payload 223 miles (360km)
Dimensions: main rotor diameter 34 ft 5½ in (10.5 m); fuselage length 31 ft 3¼ in (9.53 m); height 10 ft 5¼ in (3.18 m); main rotor disc area 931 sq ft (86.5 m²)

Standard helicopters of the Kuwaiti air force are the Aérospatiale Puma and Gazelle, one of the latter (an SA 342) being illustrated here.

Aérospatiale/Westland SA 341 Gazelle

Aérospatiale/Westland SA 342M with four HOT anti-tank missiles.

second-generation machine the US Army is buying the AH-64 Apache made by Hughes, with two 1,600-hp (1193-kW) General Electric T700 engines and a very impressive array of sensors and weapons including up to 16 Hellfire laser-guided missiles and a rapid-fire 30-mm (1.18-in) gun. Unfortunately development has taken longer than expected so that inflation has greatly increased the price, and the plan to buy 536 had to be downgraded to 446.

Firing a HOT anti-tank missile from an Aérospatiale Gazelle. This light helicopter carries four missiles, the SA 342M version being fitted with a roof-mounted sight.

No dedicated gunship has appeared in the Soviet Union, but the mass-produced Mil Mi-8, which can carry 28 troops plus devastating armament, has since 1974 been backed up by the Mi-24, called 'Hind' by NATO, which is one of the most useful tactical helicopters ever built. Whilst retaining a main cabin for eight fully equipped troops (more in emergency), it has a gunship-type forward fuselage for pilot and gunner and the greatest array of sensors and weapons of any production helicopter. These formidable machines have played a leading role in the war in Afghanistan.

Army helicopters in the West

Numerically the chief army helicopters are small and agile machines used for observation and liaison, such as the Hughes OH-6A Cayuse and simpler versions of the Hughes 500MD Defender, Bell 206 (JetRanger), Westland Scout, MBB BO 105 and Aérospatiale Gazelle and Dauphin. In the class above 2,000 hp (1491 kW) we have larger machines able to carry a platoon of men or a variety of weapons. A notable member of this class is the Westland Army Lynx, which in 1982 emerged in Mk 3 form with advanced sensors and weapons whilst retaining its ability to carry 10 troops. Much larger, the US Army Sikorsky UH-60A Blackhawk costs twice as much but carries up to 11 troops and external weapons, such as 16 Hellfire missiles. The EH-60A is an electronic-warfare model designed to intercept and study hostile communications and jam them if necessary. The EH-60B is a SOTAS (Stand-off target acquisition system) for detecting battlefield targets, but this was cancelled despite its obvious value. Largest of the current crop of assault helicopters are the British Westland Commando, with a load of 28 troops or 8,000-lb (3629-kg) cargo, and various weapon or electronic-warfare installations, and the monster Sikorsky CH-53 and HH-53 Sea Stallion and Super Jolly previously mentioned.

Mil Mi-24

History and Notes
This important combat helicopter family has dynamic parts (engines and rotors) bearing close kinship with those of the Mi-8, yet while the main rotor is considerably smaller in diameter the engines are much more powerful! The first Mi-24 version, called 'Hind-A' by NATO, was initially seen in large numbers in East Germany in 1974, and so is thought to have flown as a prototype in about 1968. Its fuselage is divided into a large cockpit area for a normal flight crew of four (pilot, co-pilot, gunner/navigator with heavy machine-gun, and forward observer) and an un-obstructed main cabin for eight fully equipped troops. On each side large wing-like weapon arms (which do in fact give lift in forward flight) slope sharply downwards and support six pylons, four of them for rocket pods, bombs or other heavy stores and the outermost carrying twin rails for a total of four AT-2 'Swatter' guided missiles for use against armour or other hard targets. Even larger numbers have been built of another model, 'Hind-D', which has a revised airframe with the tail rotor moved from the right to the left of the swept fin, and a new nose equipped for a pilot at the upper level and a weapon operator lower down in the extreme nose, and with the greatest array of tactical sensors, weapon-aiming systems, communications, EW devices and all-weather avionics ever seen on a helicopter. Well over 1,000 of many sub-types had been built by 1983, about 150 being exported to five client states.

Specification: Mil Mi-24 'Hind-D'
Origin: USSR
Type: tactical gunship helicopter
Armament: one 12.7-mm (0.5-in) four-barrel gun in remote-control turret under nose for use against ground or aerial targets; four inboard weapon pylons for various loads (usually 32-tube 57-mm/2.24-in rocket pods) and two outboard pylons for twin launch rails for AT-2 'Swatter' or AT-6 'Spiral' laser-homing anti-armour missiles
Powerplant: two 2,200-hp (1641-kW) Isotov TV3-117 turboshafts

Performance: maximum speed 215 mph (346 km/h); range with maximum weapon load 559 miles (900 km)
Weights: empty about 14,300 lb (6500 kg); maximum take-off 25,400 lb (11500 kg)
Dimensions: main rotor diameter about 55 ft 9 in (17.0 m); fuselage length 55 ft 9 in (17.0 m); height 14 ft 0 in (4.25 m); main rotor disc area 2,443.5 sq ft (227.0 m²)

Keith Fretwell

This superb illustration is certainly the most accurate yet to have appeared of any version of the Mil Mi-24, the type depicted being the so-called 'Hind-D' armed assault and anti-tank version as used by the Czech air force. Features include the kinked main-rotor blades of composite construction, held in a titanium hub, four UV-32-57 pods

(each housing 32 rockets of 57-mm/2.24-in calibre), four outboard AT-6 Spiral anti-tank missiles, foreign-object

deflectors ahead of the inlets to the 2,200-hp (1641-kW) TV3-117 engines, forward-looking IR and low-light TV sensors, four-barrel gun in a remotely-aimed turret, and long air-data sensor probe.

Distinguished by having a tractor (left-hand side) tail rotor, the Bell UH-1H is produced under licence in Japan by Fuji Heavy Industries together with the smaller Model 204B-2. Here a civil Model 205A-1 is seen airlifting materials to a remote construction site, such as are found all over Japan.

Civil Helicopters

It was natural that airlines should play with helicopters as soon as such vehicles were available, but early routes came and went. Only with the vast growth of general aviation, executive flying and offshore oil have helicopters become big commercial business.

A beautiful portrait of the Fairey Rotodyne, later the Westland Rotodyne when in 1960 the Yeovil-based company took over Fairey's helicopter programmes.

Where civil helicopters differ from army and naval models is that, in general, they have to make a profit for their operators. Thus they are perhaps even more of a challenge, despite the fact that all they have to carry are people and cargo, without special electronic fits, armour, battle protection and the other complicated mission equipment of their armed counterparts. In fact, compared with aeroplanes, helicopters are basically less efficient. They need much more power to carry a given payload, and as they also fly relatively slowly they burn much more fuel. It is therefore ridiculous to use airline helicopters to fly between airports, as has sometimes been attempted. Helicopters make economic sense only if their unrivalled convenience – for example, their ability to fly into city centres – can be reflected in fares that are much more expensive per mile than normal.

Helicopters of the World

With headquarters in Vancouver, Okanagan is one of the world's biggest commercial helicopter operators. Among its vast fleet are 12 Sikorsky S-61 passenger carriers, one being the S-61L illustrated. This was the somewhat rare version without amphibious capability.

Early helicopters were doubly uneconomic because they carried so few passengers. By 1950 services had been tried in England using the Westland WS-51 and later the Bristol 171, and various services operated briefly in the USA, but the first important airline use of helicopters was by the Belgian airline Sabena, which in 1953 opened an international network of routes centred on Brussels, at first using the six-passenger Sikorsky S-55 and later the 15-passenger Sikorsky S-58. From the early 1960s larger twin-turbine machines were used, notably the Vertol (later Boeing-Vertol) 107, which was used by New York Airways on routes linking the top of the PanAm building with various New York City airports, and the 28-passenger Sikorsky S-61L and S-61N airline versions used by many operators, including Los Angeles Airways, BEA (later British Airways) and KLM.

Airline operations

None of these helicopter networks survived, though a few small routes have proved so useful that they remain active and will continue to do so. Most are between places where there are no good airports and where surface travel is inconvenient. A typical example is the short hop between St Just (Land's End, on the English mainland) and St Mary's in the Scilly Isles. Hops between Scottish islands, however, are made more economically by fixed-wing machines, and the same is true for much more than 99 per cent of all sectors flown by the world's airlines today.

Apart from the special case of the oil industry, the only area where civil helicopters in quite large sizes are used in numbers is the Soviet Union. Here there is no need to make a profit; the costs are

Still wearing the livery of its defunct predecessor, Court Line of the UK, Court Helicopters of Cape Town, South Africa is a thriving supplier to offshore tankers and oil rigs around the coast. Two of its less-common types are the Sikorsky S-58T, with PT6T Turbo-TwinPac power (departing in the rear) and the S-62A with single T58. Both carry weather radar.

Unusual head-on aspect of a Mil Mi-17 working with a slung load, which for very short lifts can be as much as 5000 kg (11,023 lb). The Mi-17 has TV3-117MT engines of 1,900 hp (1417 kW) each, and is distinguished by a tractor (left side) tail rotor. The air-conditioning pack is not fitted (it can be attached to the front of the right external tank).

borne mainly out of taxes, so fares are set at about the same level as for fixed-wing travel or by rail. Types used include the giant Mil Mi-6, Mi-26 and the Mi-10 crane, but most are the smaller Mi-4, Mi-8, Mi-17 and the Kamov Ka-26. At least 2,000 are used for agricultural spraying and dusting, while about half the remainder are used to support development of new territories, especially those where oil has been found, as at Tyumen in Siberia. A great number of large machines are used in Siberian oilfields laying pipelines.

Where the oil is under the sea this last task cannot be done by helicopters, but they are even more essential to maintain communications between the mainland and the exploration or production platforms. All over the world oil rigs on the Continental Shelf are being sustained by large commercial helicopters which bring in personnel, food and drink, mail, medical supplies, materials

Not many of the 800-plus Mil Mi-8 helicopters operate with export civil customers, but this example is on non-scheduled work with the Polish Instal company, carrying 32 passengers or cargo. Instal expects also to acquire the more powerful Mi-17, thus removing an engine-out problem in hot-weather conditions.

Helicopters of the World

The Bell Model 222 is the first American twin-engine light helicopter, and among its operators is Helikopter Service, Oslo.

and tools, drill bits and pipes (the largest single item of cargo) and much more besides. Several oil-support operators have fleets of 50 or more helicopters, far outnumbering all other civil operators. Probably the most numerous machine on a worldwide basis is the Bell Model 205/206/212, all commercial versions of the familiar Huey. These were augmented in 1980 by the neat twin-turbine Bell Model 222, in 1981 by the Bell Model 412 with low-vibration four-blade rotor and in 1982 by the big 18-passenger Bell Model 214ST, the first offshore operator of which is British Caledonian Helicopters over the North Sea.

Oilfield support

Previously the varied fleets on oilfield support included such small machines as the Aérospatiale Alouette and Bell 47, as well as the big Sikorsky S-61 airline-type machines. Today the biggest outside the Soviet Union are the Boeing 234s, which are highly developed airline versions of the

The largest helicopter produced by Bell, the Model 214ST can accommodate 19 passengers, and is admirably suited by means of its avionics and twin-engine powerplant for the offshore support and city-centre commuter roles.

Aérospatiale/Westland SA 330J Puma of the Bristow Helicopter Group, UK, fitted with IFR weather radar.

Both of Asahi Helicopter's Aérospatiale AS 350B Ecureuil light light helicopters are seen on the pad of the Shibaura rooftop heliport in Tokyo. The type is used mainly in the air-taxi role.

Helicopters of the World

Boeing Vertol Model 234
Commercial Chinook of British
Airways Helicopters.

Chinook. The main variant is the Model 234LR (long-range), which has greatly increased fuel capacity in enlarged fuselage side fairings between the front and rear pairs of landing gears. With 45-minute reserves this model can fly 661 miles (1064 km) carrying a maximum load of 44 passengers, but in oilfield work the passengers tend to be extremely husky men who bring with them heavy kit and equipment, so it is rare to have 44 on board. Altogether the 234 is the most capable transport helicopter in the world, with the sole exception of the new Soviet Mil Mi-26, which far surpasses it.

Right: This commercial Aérospatiale AS 332C was the first of its type to be delivered, to Tyrolean Airways of Austria. This model of Super Puma seats 17 passengers, four fewer than the limit for the stretched AS 332L.

Executive helicopters

Aérospatiale, Europe's largest helicopter manufacturer, has built no fewer than 10 basic types of civil turbine helicopter, up to the 37-passenger three-engined SA 321F Super Frelon. Largest in current production is the 3,500-hp (2610-kW) Super Puma, which has sold particularly well to oilfield operators like the Puma before it. A British airline, Bristow Helicopters, bought a fleet of 35 of the long-body AS 332L model, calling them Bristow Tigers. These have enlarged windows, auto-jettison doors, larger liferafts, inflight music over the public-address system and 19 folding passenger seats. Another extremely capable machine, bought by British Airways and many other operators including the helicopter airlines of Los Angeles and San Francisco, is the Westland 30, which is more efficient and compact even than the Super Puma, carrying up to 19 passengers in great comfort in a remarkably spacious cabin on only 2,000 hp (1491 kW) (though future versions

Developed from the Lynx, the Westland 30 is a general-purpose transport helicopter for both civil and military roles. In various configurations, it can accommodate up to 17 troops, 19 passengers, 6 stretchers and various cargo loads. This example is the prototype, which first flew on 10 April 1979.

may have the General Electric CT7 engine of some 1,700 hp/1268 kW, giving almost doubled power). Later Westland 30 versions will carry 17 passengers and baggage over airline sectors longer than 350 miles (563 km) at the high cruising speed of 161 mph (259 km/h), or 13 passengers over 525-mile (845-km) sectors. Later Westland, in partnership with Agusta of Italy, expects to produce an airline version of the big EH.101 with three CT7 or T700 engines (the T700 being the military CT7 used in army or navy versions). The EH.101 will have a cabin steward and pantry to minister to 30-plus passengers on long sectors.

Below: The Kawasaki KV-107/IIA, with uprated powerplant, is used by the Saudi Arabians, who have four firefighting KV-107/IIA-SM-1s and three KV-107/IIA-SM-2s for rescue and aeromedical evacuation.

Helicopters of the World

The Aérospatiale SA 315B Lama is widely used by air-taxi operators such as Aircraft Innsbruck Luftfahrt.

Best-seller among the smaller airline and corporate (executive) helicopters is the Sikorsky S-76, which seats up to 12 and can cruise at the excellent speed of 178 mph (286 km) on two 682-hp (509-kW) Allison engines. This well-streamlined machine has set many world records including speeds up to 213 mph (343 km). Three supplied to Jordan's air force are equipped lavishly as ambulances including intensive-care kits. Many helicopters around the world are used for emergency and disaster-relief use, though few have such medical equipment. An outstanding example

An Aérospatiale Alouette III of the French Gendarmerie hovers against a mountain background. The Alouette III's high-altitude performance suits the type admirably for work (including SAR) in such regions.

A colourful MBB BO 105CB demonstrator with a slung load. Current models of this twin-turbine light helicopter are cleared for single-pilot IFR operation in temperatures from −45°C to 54°c (129°F).

is the team of 20 MBB BO 105 helicopters used in the Federal German *Katastrophenschutze* network. As early as 1975 they had saved more than 1,000 lives in 10,000 missions, and the total is now several times higher.

The twin-turbine BO 105 is one of the more expensive of the smaller executive class of helicopters, of which the most numerous are the various versions of the Bell Model 206 JetRanger. Powered by a single Allison turboshaft engine of 317 hp (236 kW) or 420 hp (313 kW), these shapely machines normally seat the pilot and a passenger in front and three passengers on a rear bench seat. The 206L LongRanger has a stretched fuselage normally seating the pilot plus six passengers, and the engine is a more powerful Allison rated at 500 hp (373 kW). Italy's even more beautiful Agusta A 109A has retractable landing gear and cruises faster than the JetRanger (up to 174 mph/280 km/h) on two 400-hp (298-kW) Allison engines, seating up to eight. Newest of the small

Agusta A 109 of the Italian police.

The Bell Model 206 JetRanger utility helicopter, used here for crop-spraying with lateral spraybars and an underfuselage tank.

Sikorsky S-76 Spirit

History and Notes

Growing demands for transport helicopters in support of offshore energy operations led Sikorsky to initiate worldwide market research to establish the requirements of such operators. An important factor to which the company needed an answer was seating capacity, and in 1975 was able to begin the development of a 14-seat commercial helicopter designated S-76 and later named Spirit. The first of four prototypes (N762SA) was flown on 13 March 1977, and the first fully certificated IFR production aircraft was delivered to Air Logistics of Lafayette, Louisiana on 27 February 1979.

This short certification programme resulted from the use of an advanced dynamic system/powerplant combination evolved for military requirements, but further development continued from the time that production began, leading to an improved S-76 Mark II from 1 March 1982. This differs by having improved cabin ventilation, dynamic system refinements, more access panels to simplify maintenance, and the introduction of an advanced version of the Allison 250 turboshaft which gives an increase in guaranteed power output. In May 1982 Sikorsky announced three other versions: a more basic S-76 Utility, S-76 Military and the S-76EMS for emergency medical service. Sales were approaching 400 in late 1982, of which about half had been delivered.

Specification: Sikorsky S-76 Mark II
Origin: United States
Type: utility transport helicopter
Accommodation: flight crew of 2; up to 12 passengers

Sikorsky S-76 Spirit; by 1983 the total sold exceeded 400.

Powerplant: two 682-shp (509-kW) Allison 250-C305 turboshafts
Performance: maximum cruising speed 167 mph (269 km/h); economic cruising speed 144 mph (232 km/h); service ceiling 15,000 ft (4570 m); range with 12 passengers and fuel reserves 465 miles (748km)
Weights: empty equipped 5,600 lb (2540 kg); maximum take-off 10,300 lb (4672 kg)
Dimensions: main rotor diameter 44 ft 0 in (13.41 m); length, rotors turning 52 ft 6 in (16.0 m); height 14 ft 5¾ in (4.41 m); main rotor disc area 1,257.0 sq ft (116.78 m²)

Sikorsky S-76 Spirit

Sikorsky S-76 Spirit company demonstrator.

Aérospatiale machines is another good-looker, the AS 350 Ecureuil (Squirrel) with six seats and a 640-hp (477-kW) engine (marketed in North America as the AStar) and the AS 355 TwinStar (in France called Ecureuil 2) with two 425-hp (317-kW) Allisons. In a larger size category come various Aérospatiale Dauphins, seating a pilot and up to 13 passengers and available with various kinds of fixed or retractable landing gear and with either a 1,050-hp (783-kW) Turboméca Astazou or two 710-hp (529-kW) Turboméca Arriel engines.

An unidentified US civil S-76 Spirit in a typical executive environment. The standard model, the S-76 Mk II, is powered by two 682-hp (509-kW) Allison C30S engines.